SQUADRONS!

No. 66

THE HANDLEY PAGE

HAMPDEN

- TORPEDO-BOMBER -

PHIL H. LISTEMANN

ISBN: 978-2-494471-16-0

Copyright

© **2024 Philedition - Phil Listemann**

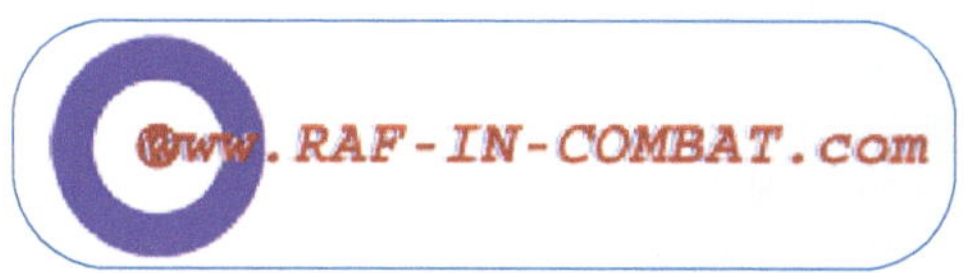

Colour profiles: Juanita Franzi/Aero Illustrations

GLOSSARY OF TERMS

PERSONEL :
(AUS)/RAF: Australian serving in the RAF
(BEL)/RAF: Belgian serving in the RAF
(CAN)/RAF: Canadian serving in the RAF
(CZ)/RAF: Czechoslovak serving in the RAF
(NFL)/RAF: Newfoundlander serving in the RAF
(NL)/RAF: Dutch serving in the RAF
(NZ)/RAF: New Zealander serving in the RAF
(POL)/RAF: Pole serving in the RAF
(RHO)/RAF: Rhodesian serving in the RAF
(SA)/RAF: South African serving in the RAF
(US)/RAF - RCAF : American serving in the RAF or RCAF

RANKS
G/C : Group Captain
W/C : Wing Commander
S/L : Squadron Leader
F/L : Flight Lieutenant
F/O : Flying Officer
P/O : Pilot Officer
W/O : Warrant Officer
F/Sgt : Flight Sergeant
Sgt : Sergeant
Cpl : Corporal
LAC : Leading Aircraftman

OTHER
ATA: Air Transport Auxiliary
CO : Commander
DFC : Distinguished Flying Cross
DFM : Distinguished Flying Medal
DSO : Distinguished Service Order
Eva. : Evaded
ORB : Operational Record Book
OTU : Operational Training Unit
PoW : Prisoner of War
PAF: Polish Air Force
RAF : Royal Air Force
RAAF : Royal Australian Air Force
RCAF : Royal Canadian Air Force
RNZAF : Royal New Zealand Air Force
SAAF : South African Air Force
s/d: Shot down
Sqn : Squadron
† : Killed

THE HANDLEY PAGE HAMPDEN

In 1932, the Air Ministry issued Specification B.9/32 seeking a twin-engine day bomber with higher performance than any preceding bomber aircraft. Handley Page and Vickers both designed aircraft to meet this specification; the Vickers design became the Wellington. The Handley Page design team drafted a radical aircraft, initially relying upon the politically favoured Rolls-Royce Goshawk engine. By mid-1934, development of the Goshawk looked less promising, and the Air Ministry relaxed the tare (unloaded) weight requirement of the specification, allowing for the use of heavier and more powerful radial engines such as the Bristol Perseus and Pegasus. The Handley Page design soon found support with the Air Ministry in part because it was judged to represent a fair compromise between range, payload and speed.

On 21 June 1936, the prototype, K4240, conducted its maiden flight powered by a pair of Bristol Pegasus P.E.5S(A) engines. In late June, the prototype was put on public display in the 'New Types Park' at the Hendon Air Show, London. In August, in response to the K4240's successful flight trials, the Air Ministry issued an initial order for 180 production aircraft (serials **L4032–L4211**) as Hampden Mk.Is. They were powered by two Bristol Pegasus XVIII nine-cylinder air-cooled radial piston engines, rated for 1,000 hp (750 kW) each at 3,000 feet; the aircraft was armed with one fixed, forward-firing 0.303 in (7.7-mm) machine gun in the nose and 3–5 Vickers K machine guns: one flexibly mounted in the nose and one or two each in dorsal and ventral positions. It could carry a 4,000-lb (1,800-kg) load of bombs or mines. Concurrently, a second order for 100 aircraft powered by the Napier Dagger was issued to Belfast-based Short & Harland; these were later denominated as Hereford Mk.Is. The serials allotted were **L6002–L6101**. A second batch of Herefords was ordered (**N9055–N9081** and **N9084–N9106**) and all had been delivered by September 1940. However, as the Dagger proved troublesome, the type never entered operational service and 24 Herefords were eventually converted to Hampdens. In the meantime, more orders were placed: 200 Hampdens built by Handley Page (**P1145–P1189, P1194–P1261, P1265–P1305** and **P1309–P1356**) then another 120 (**P4285–P4324, P4335–P4384** and **P4389–P4418**) for a grand total for Handley Page of 500; nine hundred were built by English Electric in five batches of 75, 120, 150, 425 and 120 with serials **P2062–P2100** and **P2110–P2145**, then **X2893–X2922, X2959–X3154** and, finally, **AD719–AD768, AD782–AD873, AD895–AD939, AD959–AD988, AE115–AE159, AE184–AE203, AE218–AE267, AE286–AE320** and **AE352–AE442**. The last batch received the serials **AT109–AT158** and **AT172–AT260**. This final batch built by English Electric was part of a larger one of 250 airframes but the last 130 were cancelled (AT261–AT265, AT280–AT314, AT332–AT371 and AT387–AT436) when the Air Ministry switched priority to the four-engine bombers. The Canadians participated in production of the type and 160 were built by Canadian Associated Aircraft in three batches of 80 (**P5298–P5346** and **P5386–P5436**), 12 (**AJ988–AJ999**) and 68 (**AN100–AN167**). Close to 80 Canadian-production Hampdens were kept in Canada to equip No. 32 Operational Training Unit (OTU); the rest were sent to the UK. Deliveries of the

Hampden L4032, the first production aircraft, seen in August 1938. It was never issued to an operational unit and served as a test aircraft until May 1941, then as an instructional airframe.

A torpedo is loaded into the bomb bay of a Hampden of No. 32 OTU at Sidney (British Columbia) in October 1942. The torpedo type carried for anti-shipping operations was usually the Mk.XV of 1,801 lbs (817 kgs), with a warhead of 545 lbs (247 kgs), introduced in 1942.

Hampden took place between August 1938 and March 1942 for the British production and between September 1940 and May 1942 for the Canadians. A single Hampden was delivered to Sweden in September 1938.

The Hampden entered service with No. 49 Squadron in September 1938 and 226 were in service with ten squadrons by the start of the Second World War, with six units forming the operational strength of No. 5 Group of Bomber Command in Lincolnshire. The Hampden was used as a bomber with Bomber Command until September 1942. More than 15,500 sorties were flown in three years of operations. The torpedo-bomber version was only basically different from the original production aircraft in that the bomb bay and lower gunner's position were modified to allow a torpedo to be carried. Trials were conducted during 1941. The operational life of the Hampden as a bomber was coming to an end with the introduction of the four-engine bombers so it was a good way for the type to have a second life on the front line. An initial batch of 40 Hampdens were converted and delivered by the end of March 1942, enough to equip two squadrons (initially Nos 415 RCAF and 489 (NZ) Squadrons). To respond to Coastal Command's needs, two of No 5 Group's Hampden squadrons, Nos 144 and 455 (RAAF), were selected to transfer to the Coastal Command; this became effective on 21 April. Consequently, more Hampdens were needed and conversions continued in 1942 and 1943; in all, 290 Hampdens were converted to torpedo-bomber configuration.

No. 144 Squadron (code: PL)

A pre-war RAF bomber squadron, No. 144 Squadron converted to the Hampden in March 1939. It flew its first war operation on 26 September 1939 and was regularly engaged until April 1942 when the squadron's role was changed to torpedo bombing. It joined Coastal Command and arrived at its new base, Leuchars, on the 21st; its final sorties for Bomber Command were carried out on the 16th. Having yet to receive the torpedo-bomber variant of the Hampden, 144 continued to send bombers on night operations, three being dispatched on the night of 4/5 May. Sadly, one aircraft, AT188, captained by Sgt J Long (RCAF), failed to return. That was the first Hampden loss for Coastal Command.

Intensive training was performed in June under the supervision of Wing Commander J McLaughlin, the CO. Close to 500 hours were eventually flown; training continued in July with 640 hours flown despite the weather, especially at Wick where 144 was detached from the 17th. On 27 July, the squadron carried out its first sorties with Hampden torpedo bombers, 12 aircraft heading to Norway for a shipping strike. Two torpedoes were dropped, one by the CO and the second by P/O H.J.W. Bowden, on two German destroyers west of Kristiansand Fjord. No hits were recorded. These would be the only sorties from Wick as, on 3 August, 144 returned to Leuchars. For the rest of the month, no operational sorties were achieved as the focus was on training. That month, it was decided 144, with No. 455 (RAAF) Squadron, would be sent to northern Russia to help protect the Arctic convoys. While four Hampdens remained at Leuchars for training purposes, 16 took off on 4 September for Vaenga via Afrikanda. Things did not go as planned. Three Hampdens never reached Afrikanda and were all posted as missing. It was later learned two were intercepted by German fighters near Petsamo, in Finland, one crew being captured while the other crew was posted missing, although Sgt J.C.R. Bray was also captured. The third crashed near Petsamo and only the captain, P/O E.H.E. Perry, survived as a PoW. Then, arriving at Afrikanda, Hampden AE310, captained by E.H.D. Nelson, crashed near the base, but the crew managed to escape serious injury. Another Hampden did not make it; P/O D.I. Evans, in AE436, experienced an engine failure and was forced to make an emergency landing on a mountain. Three crewmembers were killed; two others, including Evans, managed to reach Sweden from where they were later evacuated to England. Another incident was also recorded when the Hampden captained by Sgt W.H. Hood was attacked by Russian fighters, killing the lower rear gunner, Sgt W.T. Tabor of the RCAF, in the process. The remaining Hampdens continued their journey and reached Vaenga on the 6th. A single sortie was carried out on 14 September with 11 Hampdens, but no enemy units were seen and all aircraft returned to base after seven-and-a-half hours in the air. During the first three weeks of October, the aircrew remained on standby but nothing happened. Finally, on 22 October, the entire detachment embarked on HMS *Argonaut* for Britain, leaving the aircraft behind for the Soviets.

In the meantime, at Leuchars, three anti-submarine patrols were carried out on the 21st, followed by three more on the 23rd, from Sumburgh this time where the aircraft were on detachment. Ten more would follow by the end of the month. Early in November, 144 was reunited at Leuchars but operations remained at a low tempo with mostly nuisance raids over Norway and some anti-submarine patrols being flown. One Hampden failed to return from a nuisance raid on the 22nd, the entire crew being posted as missing. In December, 144 logged 27 sorties; on the 13th, it managed to damage a 4,000-ton merchant ship off the Norwegian coast with a torpedo, but an escorting flak ship hit the aircraft captained by P/O H.J. Stillborn (RCAF) whose crew was posted missing after the Hampden was seen to hit the sea. Hampden P1250 (F/L Bowden) met the same fate but three of the crew survived as prisoners of war.

In January 1943, about 20 shipping-strike sorties were performed, but all were unsuccessful. However, on 15 January, two Hampdens flown by P/O Walker and F/Sgt S.C. Price were attacked by a single Ar196; the combat proved inconclusive. Operations continued until 18 January, then, the squadron was taken off the front line the next day to be re-equipped with Beaufighters. In all, 144 Squadron logged 110 sorties with Hampdens while with Coastal Command.

The surviving Hampdens of the Russian detachment were eventually handed over to the Soviets who used them until the end of 1943.

Summary of the aircraft lost on Operations - 144 Squadron

Date of TO	Crew	S/N	Origin	Serial	Code	Fate
22.11.42	S/L John R.D. **HIRD**	RAF No. 37852	RAF	**P2063**		†
	Sgt Davidson W. **HEPPLEWHITE**	RAF No. 1189303	RAF			†
	Sgt Robert J. **COLES**	RAF No. 1310109	RAF			†
	Sgt Raymond H. **ALVEY**	RAF No. 755235	RAF			†
13.12.42	F/L Huie J.W. **BOWDEN**	RAF No. 47002	RAF	**P1250**	PL-M	**PoW**
	F/O Joseph L. **MENNILL**	CAN./ J.7216	RCAF			**PoW**
	Sgt Jack **VOSPER**	RAF No. 1360578	RAF			†
	Sgt Cyril D. **ELSMORE**	RAF No. 1311071	RAF			**PoW**
	F/Sgt John H. **STILBORN**	CAN./ R.85220	RCAF	**P4373**	PL-R	†
	F/Sgt John W. **SPROULE**	CAN./ R.76630	RCAF			†
	Sgt Harry F. **DELL**	RAF No. 963398	RAF			†
	Sgt George H. **FOSTER**	RAF No. 932201	RAF			†

Total: 3

Hampden AE436/PL-J taken in flight while 144 was still serving as a bomber squadron and was lost in September 1942 while on transit to Russia.

Summary of the aircraft lost by accident - 144 Squadron

Date of TO	Crew	S/N	Origin	Serial	Code	Fate
04.09.42	Sgt Henry L. **BERTRAND**	RAF No. 1077247	RAF	**P1273**	PL-Q	**PoW**
	Sgt Edward D. **BIND**	CAN./ R.69862	RCAF			**PoW**
	Sgt Kenneth S. **PIPER**	CAN./ R.74851	RCAF			**PoW**
	Sgt Kenneth C. **SMITH**	CAN./ R.79571	RCAF			**PoW**
	Cpl George R. **DESFORGES***	RAF No. 1269515	RAF			**PoW**
	P/O Esmond H.E. **PERRY**	RAF No. 110845	RAF	**P1344**	PL-K	**PoW**
	Sgt Gordon E. **MILLER**	CAN./ R.88850	RCAF			†
	Sgt James M. **ROBERTSON**	RAF No. 1021461	RAF			†
	Sgt Daniel C. **GARRITY**	RAF No. 1061251	RAF			†
	Cpl Christopher G. **SHEPHERD***	RAF No. 1009075	RAF			**PoW**
	Sgt Eric H.D. **NELSON**	RAF No. 1378842	RAF	**AE310**		-
	Sgt Walter K. **McGREGOR**	CAN./ R.68723	RCAF			-
	Sgt John **KANE**	RAF No. 1309277	RAF			-
	Sgt George H. **FOSTER**	RAF No. 932201	RAF			-
	Cpl **NORTH***	RAF No. ?	RAF			-
	Sgt Walter H. **HOOD**	CAN./ R.77067	RCAF	**AE356**		-
	Sgt Donald Y. **TURNBULL**	CAN./ R.83017	RCAF			-
	Sgt Robert J. **O'NEIL**	CAN./ R.67741	RCAF			-
	Sgt Walter T. **TABOR**	CAN./ R.51583	RCAF			†
	Cpl **BARKER***	RAF No. ?	RAF			-
	P/O David I. **EVANS**	RAF No. 108570	RAF	**AE436**	PL-J	**Int.**
	P/O William H. **BOWDEN**	CAN./ J.7210	RCAF			†
	Sgt John P. **CAMPBELL**	CAN./ R.69686	RCAF			†
	Sgt James S. **JEWITT**	CAN./ R.56296	RCAF			†
	Cpl Bernard J. **SOWERBY***	RAF No. 1063437	RAF			**Int.**
	Sgt John C. **BRAY**	RAF No. 1384708	RAF	**AT138**		**PoW**
	Sgt John D. **SMITH**	RAF No. 920973	RAF			†
	Sgt Roy S. **OTTER**	RAF No. 950301	RAF			†
	Sgt George D. **KIRBY**	RAF No. 1181778	RAF			†
	AC2 Leslie H. **MALLINSON***	RAF No. 1476073	RAF			†

*Groundcrew

Total: 6

Ships claims - confirmed or probable: 2 *(ca. 10,000 tons)*
A/S patrols, hours flown: 1,120

First operational sortie:
27.04.42
Last operational sortie:
23.09.43

Number of sorties: 535

Total aircraft written-off: 42

Aircraft lost on operations: 28
Aircraft lost in accidents: 14

Squadron code letters:

GX (up to end 1942)

COMMANDING OFFICERS

W/C Edgar L. WUTERLE	RAF No. 37220	(CAN)/RAF	...	30.07.42
W/C Ronald R. DENNIS	CAN./ C.847	RCAF	30.07.42	10.11.42
W/C Wilfred W. BEAN	CAN./ C.1071	RCAF	10.11.42	15.03.43
W/C George H.D. EVANS	RAF No. 33309	RAF	15.03.43	01.08.43
W/C Charles G. RUTTAN	CAN./ C.871	RCAF	01.08.43	...

SQUADRON USAGE

Formed in August 1941, No. 415 Squadron was, from the start, a torpedo-bomber unit under the authority of Coastal Command. It was initially equipped with Bristol Beauforts and Blenheims, working up with these, but never became operational because of a lack of the former type. Logically, re-equipment with torpedo-bomber Hampdens was undertaken at Thorney Island when the type was adopted by the RAF and conversion began in January 1942. The squadron was, at the time, commanded by W/C 'Wally' Wurtele, a Canadian serving in the RAF and the first Hampden was taken on charge on 21 January. The remaining Hampdens allocated to the squadron arrived in February, all being on charge by the middle of the month. Training commenced on the type; the first incident occurred when AT248/J crashed on take-off on the 9th. Fortunately, none of the aircrew was injured. However, three days later, AT248/W failed to return from a training exercise, the crew being posted missing. Another crew perished soon after when AT230/L spun into a hill near Hambleton. The squadron became operational at the end of April and the first ops were flown on the 27th with three anti-submarine patrols carried out by three Hampdens from St. Eval, the CO flying one of the aircraft. This effort was repeated the next day. Anti-submarine patrols remained the main task in May, 415 returning to Thorney Island in mid-May. A detachment was sent to North Coates on the 27th and, two days later, the first shipping strike with bombs was carried out off the Dutch coast, from which one Hampden, AT236/R, failed to return. All four crewmen were posted missing. Another shipping strike was flown the next day with three Hampdens. Soon after, on 5 June, the squadron moved to North Coates. Sadly, just before the move, on the 4th, AT240/D failed to return from a shipping patrol; only the pilot, P/O Fredrick H 'Hoke' Mahn, an American serving in the RCAF, was rescued a fortnight later alone in a life raft. While Mahn survived, he was badly injured and had to have both legs amputated below the knees. At North Coates, 415 resumed its anti-shipping strikes. Six ops were launched in June, but attrition was severe: Hampdens AT242/F and P1153/V were both shot down into the sea between Rottum and Borkum by shipborne flak during the nights of 25/26 and 27/28 June respectively; both crews were posted missing. Eight shipping strikes were carried out in July, the first on the first night of the month. A convoy was attacked off the Frisian coast and two torpedoes launched but no results were recorded. One Hampden failed to return; AT235/P was lost with its entire crew. The squadron sustained another loss on 30 July when AD762/J had to return early with an overheating engine. The captain, W/O Bud DR McComb, requested permission to land but before any action could be taken, the Hampden crashed on the shore south of North Coates and caught fire; nobody managed to escape the burning aircraft. August saw many changes take place. A move was made to Wick on 6 August while, the same day, S/L R.R. Dennis took over the squadron from W/C Wuterle, who was posted to Canada. With the move, no operations were achieved before the 10th. That day, a formation of five Hampdens took off from Leuchars, which was now serving as a base for detachments, on an anti-shipping strike against major naval units off the coast

The first two 415's COs were Wing Commanders E.L. Wurtele (left) and R.R. Dennis (right).
Wuterle went to England in 1935 where he enlisted in the RAF. Began his career as a flight pilot with No 1 Squadron, then he was transferred to the Fleet Air Arm to fly Swordfishes, later becoming a flying instructor. In 1939, he returned to an operational squadron, No 86 with which he flew mainly convoy escorts. In August 1941, he was given command of No 415 (RCAF) Squadron on formation, and remained at the head of 415 until the end of July 1942. He was then posted back to Canada as the Chief Instructor at the RAF No 32 OTU, where he was later promoted to Group Captain and took command of the school, leaving early in 1944 ate the time he was transferred to the RCAF but no more operational appointments followed until the end of the war. He continued to served after the war.
Dennis enlisted in the RCAF in July 1938, and served with a bomber-reconnaissance squadron when war broke out. In 1941, he sailed for the UK and was posted to 415 on formation in August 1941 becoming soon after a flight commander taking eventually command of 415 between August and November 1942. Repatriated to Canada, he was given command of a new squadron in January 1943, No 149, flying Beauforts. He commanded 149 until the squadron was disbanded in March 1944. No more operational positions followed until the end of the war.

of Norway. Less than ten minutes after take-off, the Hampden flown by the newly promoted W/C Dennis crashed into the sea after the right engine experienced trouble. Fortunately, the crew managed to get into their dinghy and were rescued soon after as the other Hampdens circled protectively. During this phase, one of the aircraft had an engine overheat, forcing the pilot, P/O Cross, to return to base where he crashed on landing; the Hampden overshot and went over an embarkment at the end of the runway. Amazingly, the torpedo did not explode during the crash and nobody was hurt. Meanwhile, the rest of the formation eventually abandoned the op and returned safely to base. With what happened on the 10th and the two engine failures, an investigation was ordered and no offensive sorties were flown for the rest of August, the squadron focusing on training. This situation lasted until 15 September when half a dozen Hampdens were dispatched for an air-sea-rescue patrol which proved unsuccessful. Two days later, four Hampdens were sent on a special reconnaissance over the North Sea, an effort repeated on the 19th with two aircraft, the final operational sorties of the month. No torpedo-carrying sorties were carried out in September. Continuing its intensive training, 415 lost a Hampden and its English crew on the 24th when AT233, captained by Sgt K. Coates, was seen to lose control while flying formation practice. Another Hampden was lost in a non-operational accident on 4 October; AE360/H was posted missing with its crew while on a night navigational exercise. After another air-sea-rescue patrol the next day, 415 returned to its main task, night anti-shipping strikes, on 24 October with four operations in a row (24th, 25th, 26th and 27th). All Hampdens except one returned to base with their torpedoes; that aircraft was seen to ditch after engine and instrument trouble on the 27th. The pilot was slightly injured. In November, W/C Dennis was repatriated to Canada and replaced by S/L W.W. Bean, who was promoted to temporary wing commander at the same time. In the meantime, the squadron sustained another operational loss when AT193/R crashed in flames while returning from a night patrol over the Bay of Biscay; the aircraft hit a lorry on landing in fog and caught fire. The pilot was killed while the other crewmen suffered burns to their face and hands. On the 6th, a convoy was attacked with torpedoes in the Bay of Biscay but results could not be observed. The same result occurred the next day off the French coast but, this time, one Hampden failed to return from the daylight sortie; the aircraft was last seen with one engine on fire during the attack. It was later learned the crew had been captured and sent to a prisoner-of-war camp. Losses continued with a Hampden and crew failing to return from an anti-shipping strike off the Dutch coast on 20/21 November; bad weather was considered the probable cause for this loss. In December, a detachment was sent to Predannack but few sorties were carried out that month – just eight for 55 operational hours. One attack produced a result as 415 returned on the 22nd with a possible hit off the Dutch coast credited to the CO. The year ended with another incident when a Fortress and a Hampden, piloted by Sgt Donald, collided on the ground while

AE201/GX-Q at dispersal at Thorney Island. This aircraft was eventually destroyed when P2065 blew up on 26 February 1943.

taxiing at Thorney Island. The new year still brought no luck as January 1943 proved little better with just two anti-shipping strikes and a single torpedo dropped (it missed its target). The Predannack detachment returned in the middle of the month. While January was thankfully free of any loss, February was a different matter despite only 20 sorties being carried out. On 18 February, AE435/U crashed on take-off for an anti-shipping strike, killing the crew. It proved a fateful operation as P1157/O failed to return. It was hit by flak off the Dutch coast and ditched. The crew was lucky to survive and be rescued two days later by a Walrus. Bad luck continued for 415 when one of its Hampdens caught fire while being refueled on the 26th; two 500-lb bombs, which were in the process of being loaded on the aircraft at the time, exploded during the fire, finishing off the Hampden but also destroying another nearby. Fortunately, no casualties were recorded. In March, a detachment was sent to Tain but the month was a black one for the squadron. With a similar number of sorties as February, three Hampdens were lost in action and another in an accident: AT114/D failed to return from an anti-shipping patrol on the 11th; AE418/B crashed on approach to Thorney Island on return from a night strike; and AE395/S was shot down by flak off the Dutch coast while, earlier in the day, Wing Commander G.H.D. Evans, who had just taken command of the squadron, crashed in AT232/A during an air test after the Hampden stalled. All on board survived, although Evans was slightly injured. For the three crews lost in action, they were either killed or posted missing in action. Only three survived as prisoners of war. April continued the unit's bad run when, on the 3rd, L4084, which was on a fighter-affiliation exercise, got into a spin from which it did not recover; the crew perished. Later in the month, other casualties were recorded during another training flight when AT244/M collided with a Spitfire near Tangmere and crashed. One airman died and five were injured, including two Air Training Corps cadets. On the operational side, 175 operational hours were carried out across 36 sorties for the cost of two aircraft. On 10 April, five Hampdens were detailed for an anti-shipping strike against a convoy off Brittany (one 8,000-ton merchant ship, one destroyer and three patrol boats). Flak was intense and Hampden P1151/P was shot down close to the convoy. The crew, captained by F/Sgt G.A. Cline, was posted missing. The other Hampdens returned to base, all having been hit during what was otherwise an unsuccessful attack. The strike carried out four days later produced a better result as 415 returned to base with one 6,000-ton merchant ship possibly sunk off the Dutch coast. Weather was relatively good in May, allowing the Canadians to achieve 175 operational hours across about 30 sorties. One vessel of 4,000 tons was claimed as at least damaged, possibly sunk, on the 17th off the Dutch coast by a torpedo dropped from the Hampden captained by F/O P.M. Harris. Results could not be observed, however, as the Hampden was obliged to take evasive action to avoid flak. A great amount of smoke or steam was seen over the target. The cost was high, though, as two crews failed to return (L6055/D and AN153/B), both shot down by flak. One of the Hampdens was manned by one of the few non-Canadian crews serving with 415. June also saw tragic losses, starting with a mid-air collision between two Hampdens during a practice flight in the vicinity of the aerodrome. One crew perished while the other survived, the pilot managing to crash land at Tain. Three days later, another crew was posted missing over the Bay of Biscay, then, on 22 June, while returning from an anti-submarine patrol (the main tasking of the month), N9096/Y swung on landing and crashed into X3061/T which eventually caught fire and burnt out. Two other Hampdens were also damaged; X3115 was later found to be unrepairable and struck off charge. Fortunately, there were no casualties, but the Hampdens were only good for scrap. On 26 June, loaded with depth charges for an anti-submarine patrol, P1313/D ran out of petrol ten miles from base. Guns, ammunition, depth charges, and anything else not bolted down, were jettisoned and the pilot, Sgt K.T. Ashfield, was preparing to ditch when the left engine picked up at 300 feet. That was enough for the Hampden to make St. Merryn where it crashed wheels up. No one was hurt, but the aircraft was a write-off. Misfortune had certainly settled in for a long stay with the squadron. In July, 415 switched to anti-submarine patrols, although anti-shipping sorties were flown in the middle of the month. For the former, the Hampdens were loaded with six depth charges. While the anti-submarine patrols were relatively safe, anti-shipping strikes remained a risky undertaking with a Hampden failing to return from a night strike over the Bay of Biscay on the 16th. Another crew was posted missing on an anti-shipping patrol on the 26th, the Hampdens being loaded with bombs this time. In August, a change of command took place, W/C Evans relinquishing command to S/L C.G. Ruttan. August saw anti-submarine patrols alternating with anti-shipping patrols. On the 2nd, P/O W.R.R. Savage's crew used up a lot of their luck when, during an anti-submarine patrol, they were intercepted by five Ju88s. The combat lasted 20 minutes, the gunners firing all they could with determination, hitting all the Junkers; surprisingly, the Hampden managed to get back to St. Eval with holes throughout the fuselage and mainplane, elevators damaged, petrol tanks punctured, but no one on board injured! The same day, S/L Ruttan attacked a U-boat, dropping the six depth charges from 100 feet as the gunners fired at the U-boat. The attack was inconclusive, but a Liberator soon arrived to finish the job. Other crews were not so fortunate. P1258/R failed to return from an anti-shipping strike on the 15th, as did X2898/U; its crew was eventually taken prisoner on the 19th. The crew of AT135/S experienced engine failures during an anti-submarine patrol and had to ditch. They were rescued 45 minutes later. On 8 September, 415 was advised it would soon convert to Vickers Wellingtons and Fairey Albacores. Training, however, continued on Hampdens for the entire month. On 6 September, 415 lost four members killed on a night minelaying training exercise in L4076. Three days later, another crew was lost during a routine test flight; the Hampden was seen to crash and burn a few miles from the aerodrome. Otherwise, 415 flew its last operational sorties in September, all but a few being anti-shipping strikes. The very last Hampden op was flown on the 23rd. A final loss was recorded on the 14th when AE192/T, returning from an op, had its undercarriage collapse on landing. No one was hurt but, as the type was being withdrawn, no repairs were undertaken; the Hampden was eventually struck off charge in February 1944. As the new mounts began to arrive, the Hampdens began to leave the squadron; four remained on hand at the end of October and just one in November. This final Hampden, used as a squadron hack, stayed on charge until March 1944.

Hampden AT236/GX-R flying along the West Sussex coast in the spring of 1942. No. 415 Squadron was based at Thorney Island at the time. AT236 was lost on a shipping strike off the Frisian islands on the night of 29/30 May. The crew perished. *(Andrew Thomas)*

Above the last three 415's COs of the Hampden era:

Left W/C W.W. Bean who led 415 between November and March 1943. He enlisted in the RCAF in May 1939 and initially served in Canada before to be sent overseas in July 1941 to join 415 on formation, taking over A Flight in February 1942. On completion of his tour as Commanding Officer, he was repatriated to Canada and served in various HQ positions until the end of war. Continuing his career with the RCAF, he eventually left the service with the rank of Air Vice-Marshall in 1968. In the Middle, W/C G.H.D. Evans, the only British officer of the Hampden era. A regular RAF officer he served with Nos 59 and 489 (NZ) Squadrons before joining 415 with the DFC received for his service with 489. He left 415 in August 1943 and was made Companion of the DSO in October. Right, W/C C.G. Ruttan. He joined the RCAF in 1938 and served in Canada with Nos 119 and 10 Squadrons, RCAF. In April 1943, he was posted overseas and appointed Commanding Officer of 415 Squadron which convert onto the Beaufighter at the end of 1943, leaving eventually 415 in July 1943. In the meantime, he had been made Companion of the DSO.

Confirmed claims against ships - 415 (RCAF) Squadron

Date	Captains	SN	Origin	tons	Serial	Code	Nb	Cat.
14.04.43	F/O Peter N. **Harris**	RAF No. 122954	RAF	6,000	**AN153**	B	1.0	P
	P/O Keith C. **Wathen**	Aus. 401004	RAAF			K		
17.05.43	F/L William H. **Adams**	Can./ J.5783	RCAF	4,000	**X2898**	U	1.0	P
	F/O Peter N. **Harris**	RAF No. 122954	RAF			M		
	Sgt William G. **Pilkington**	Can./ R.102781	RCAF			H		

Total: 2.0

Flight Lieutenant Adams (2nd from left) and his crew. On his right F/Sgt W.G. Metcalfe, and on his left, F/Sgt T.A. LeBlanc and P/O P.F. Sutton. This photo was taken in Canada while the crew was still in formation at 32 OTU.

Date (TO)	Crew	S/N	Origin	Serial	Code	Fate
29.05.42	P/O David H. **Sargent**	Can./ J.5670	RCAF	**AT236**	GX-R	†
	P/O Medwyn **Edwards**	Can./ R.7790	RCAF			†
	Sgt Arnold F. **Conway**	Can./ R.68413	RCAF			†
	Sgt John A. **McWilliams**	Can./ R.67152	RCAF			†
04.06.42	P/O Frederick H. **Mahn**	Can./ J.5671	(US)/RCAF	**AT240**	GX-D	**Inj.**
	F/Sgt James W. **Stirling**	Can./ R.67851	RCAF			†
	Sgt Edward **Thomas**	Can./ R.70743	RCAF			†
	Sgt William **Peebles**	Can./ R.60374	RCAF			†
24.06.42	F/Sgt James A. **Ridley**	Can./ R.60343	RCAF	**AT242**	GX-F	†
	F/Sgt Roger W. **Veit**	Can./ R.75703	RCAF			†
	Sgt Gordon D. **Klarner**	Can./ R.61191	RCAF			†
	Sgt Hugh A. **Clarson**	Can./ R.77218	RCAF			†
27.06.42	F/Sgt Irvine W. **Garfin**	Can./ R.61116	RCAF	**AT245**	GX-U	†
	Sgt Vincent B. **Whelpley**	Can./ R.73182	RCAF			†
	Sgt Douglas **Pearce**	Can./ R.79687	RCAF			†
	Sgt Boyd A. **Dakin**	Can./ R.76026	RCAF			†
	F/Sgt James **McCullum**	Can./ R.77265	RCAF	**P1153**	GX-V	†
	Sgt Henry F. **Hasleden**	Can./ R.78247	RCAF			†
	Sgt Ross M. **Neil**	Can./ R.75145	RCAF			†
	Sgt Lawrence H. **Latimer**	Can./ R.67067	RCAF			†
01.07.42	F/O Gerald G.O. **James**	Can./ J.4107	RCAF	**AT235**	GX-P	†
	Sgt Arthur K. **Farnie**	Can./ R.86310	RCAF			†
	Sgt Gordon A. **Pearce**	Can./ R.70960	RCAF			†
	Sgt Thomas **Gibbons**	Can./ R.79804	RCAF			†
30.07.42	W/OII Bud D.R. **McComb**	Can./ R.60462	RCAF	**AD762**	GX-J	†
	F/Sgt Mandel **Bloomfield**	Can./ R.61005	RCAF			†
	Sgt Roy M. **Ennis**	Can./ R.68044	RCAF			†
	Sgt John H. **Labelle**	Can./ R.74876	RCAF			†
10.08.42	W/C Ronald R. **Dennis**	Can./ C.847	RCAF	**AN124**	GX-M	-
	P/O Norman **Altstedter**	Can./ J.8134	RCAF			-
	P/O Percy A. **Houldsworth**	Can./ J.6848	RCAF			-
	Sgt Douglas A. **Stallard**	Can./ R.76517	RCAF			-
	P/O Clifford D. **Cross**	Can./ J.10826	RCAF	**AT229**	GX-V	-
	P/O William H. **Main**	Can./ J.9920	RCAF			-
	Sgt George K. **Summers**	Can./ R.78747	RCAF			-
	Sgt Reuben **Zumar**	Can./ R.74237	RCAF			-
27.10.42	F/L George H. **Lawrence**	Can./ J.5674	RCAF	**P5394**	GX-O	-
	P/O Kenneth R. **Maffre**	Can./ J.7205	RCAF			-
	P/O Lorne S. **Sharp**	Can./ J.15449	RCAF			-
	F/Sgt Reginald E. **Vokey**	Can./ R.56326	RCAF			-
01.11.42	F/O John N. **Godfrey**	Can./ J.5815	RCAF	**AT193**	GX-R	†
	P/O Ralph G. **Frederick**	Can./ J.8125	RCAF			-
	F/Sgt David M. **Coates**	Can./ R.78103	RCAF			-
	Sgt Roy A. **Clark**	Can./ R.65425	RCAF			-
07.11.42	P/O Robert F. **McBride**	Can./ J.15547	RCAF	**AT241**	GX-F	**PoW**
	P/O Alexander M.H. **Robertson**	Can./ J.15534	RCAF			**PoW**
	P/O Paul A. **Ramage**	Can./ J.15446	RCAF			**PoW**
	Sgt Gordon W. **Clubb**	Can./ R.80324	RCAF			**PoW**

Date	Name	Number	Force	Aircraft	Code	
20.11.42	Sgt Arthur J. **Tippett**	Aus. 401162	RAAF	**N9106**	GX-N	†
	P/O John J. **Lynn**	RAF No. 120916	RAF			†
	Sgt Douglas L.G. **Millar**	NZ411086	RNZAF			†
	Sgt Ronald R.T. **Sleep**	NZ411794	RNZAF			†
18.02.43	Sgt Paul B. **Campbell**	Can./ R.99129	RCAF	**AE435**	GX-U	†
	F/O Kenneth R. **Maffre**	Can./ J.7205	RCAF			†
	F/Sgt Reginald E. **Vokey**	Can./ R.56326	RCAF			†
	Sgt Zina M. **Niblock**	Can./ R.82624	RCAF			†
	F/O Alfred B. **Brenner**	Can./ J.7619	RCAF	**P1157**	GX-O	-
	F/Sgt Edward L.L. **Rowe**	Can./ J.18597	RCAF			-
	Sgt Allison **Glass**	Can./ R.86252	RCAF			-
	Sgt Eric A. **Vautier**	RAF No. 552250	RAF			-
11.03.43	W/OII Joseph N. **Reigate**	Can./ R.102772	RCAF	**AT114**	(GX)-D	†
	Sgt David T. **Hodgson**	RAF No. 1149194	(IRL)/RAF			†
	F/Sgt James H.M. **Ker**	Can./ R.90322	RCAF			†
	F/Sgt J.A. Edouard **St-Laurent**	Can./ R.55879	RCAF			†
19.03.43	Sgt William L. **Hurl**	Can./ R.102407	RCAF	**AE418**	(GX)-B	†
	P/O Barry A. **Johnson**	RAF No. 120132	RAF			†
	Sgt Walter C. **Foerster**	Can./ R.105695	RCAF			†
	Sgt Robert H. **O'Brien**	Can./ R.110081	RCAF			†
23.03.43	F/O Jospeh D.P. **McLeod**	Can./ J.10589	RCAF	**AE395**	(GX)-S	PoW
	P/O Clarke M. **Chambers**	Can./ J.12281	RCAF			†
	P/O Douglas H. **Wraith**	Can./ J.12632	RCAF			PoW
	Sgt William H.E. **Haddock**	Can./ R.106995	RCAF			PoW
10.04.43	F/Sgt Gordon A. **Cline**	Can./ R.106223	RCAF	**P1151**	(GX)-P	†
	P/O Wilfred B. **Keown**	RAF No. 120133	RAF			†
	W/OII Alexander M.J. **Kelly**	Can./ R.82376	RCAF			†
	Sgt John M. **Ryan**	NZ412357	RNZAF			†
17.05.43	P/O Keith C. **Wathen**	Aus. 401004	RAAF	**L6055**	(GX)-D	†
	F/O John M. **Crawford**	RAF No. 120922	RAF			†
	Sgt Ian M. **Sykes**	NZ413786	RNZAF			†
	Sgt Jabez H. **Steward**	RAF No. 1291128	RAF			†
	F/Sgt Lawrence E. **McGee**	Can./ R.89530	(US)/RCAF	**AN153**	(GX)-B	†
	F/O Leonard G. **Burgess**	RAF No. 117719	RAF			†
	Sgt Edward J. **Ramey**	Can./ R.73316	RCAF			†
	Sgt George B. **Jackson**	Can./ R.83435	RCAF			†
14.06.43	S/L James G. **Stronach**	Can./ J.5665	RCAF	**X2961**	(GX)-S	†
	W/OII Woodrow A. **Trask**	Can./ R.75044	RCAF			†
	F/O George K. **Crummy**	Can./ J.15612	RCAF			†
	P/O Alan B. **Clegg**	Can./ J.16173	RCAF			†
22.06.43	Sgt Alvin F. **Hildebrandt**	Can./ R.107137	RCAF	**N9096**	(GX)-Y	-
	F/Sgt Wilfred E. **MacCausland**	Can./ J.18066	RCAF			-
	Sgt Norman A.S. **Hastings**	Can./ J.18556	RCAF			-
	Sgt Wallace K. **Mailman**	Can./ R.76433	RCAF			-
16.07.43	F/Sgt Rowland **Walter**	RAF No. 1313634	RAF	**X3145**	(GX)-F	†
	F/O Vivian C.J. **Steer**	RAF No. 129403	RAF			†
	F/Sgt Harry A. **Huntington**	Can./ R.107329	RCAF			†
	F/Sgt Joseph L.L. **Janisse**	Can./ R.109971	RCAF			†
26.07.43	F/Sgt Robert **Grainger**	RAF No. 1332260	RAF	**P5301**	(GX)-D	†
	Sgt Allan **Millican**	RAF No. 1148272	RAF			†
	Sgt Ronald B. **MacKenzie**	Can./ R.99126	RCAF			†
	F/Sgt Thomas A. **Ivey**	Can./ R.119205	RCAF			†
15.08.43	S/L Peter N. **Harris**	RAF No. 122954	RAF	**P1258**	(GX)-R	†
	P/O Raymond V. **Proctor**	RAF No. 146449	RAF			†
	F/Sgt Albert G. **Innes**	RAF No. 551400	RAF			†
	F/L John O. **Bostock**	RAF No. 77530	RAF			†
18.08.43	F/O Ronald **Armstrong**	RAF No. 119120	RAF	**AT135**	(GX)-S	-
	F/O Hugh R.D.S. **Cuddon**	RAF No. 125608	RAF			-

	F/Sgt Anthony T.J.S. **Maher**	Can./ R.55787	RCAF			-
	Sgt John **Bileski**	Can./ R.94977	RCAF			-
19.08.43	F/Sgt Wilfrid A. **Robson**	RAF No. 956452	RAF	X2898	(GX)-U	**PoW**
	F/Sgt Herbert G. **Laverick**	RAF No. 1138484	RAF			**PoW**
	F/Sgt Herbert G. **Gnam**	Can./ R.131643	RCAF			**PoW**
	Sgt Harvey E. **St-Jean**	Can./ R.115726	RCAF			**PoW**

Total: 28

A Canadian crew posing on return after a running battle with six Jus88s whilst on anti-submarine patrol over the Bay of Biscay. Left to right, F/O F.A. Brockwell (Nav, RAF), P/O W.R.R. Savage (pilot, RCAF), Sgt S.J. Babyn (A/G, RCAF) and Sgt J.E. Mason (A/G, RCAF)

Date (TO)	Crew	S/N	Origin	Serial	Code	Fate
12.03.42	P/O Joseph R. **Hebert**	Can./ J.5672	RCAF	**AT247**	GX-W	†
	F/O William L. **Mackay**	Can./ R.56394	RCAF			†
	Sgt Arthur T. **Murtha**	Can./ R.73763	RCAF			†
	Sgt Harold R. **Hatfield**	Can./ R.63017	RCAF			†
23.03.42	F/Sgt Clyde H. **Jay**	Can./ R.74713	(US)/RCAF	**AT230**	GX-L	†
	Sgt Patrick G. **O'Brien**	Can./ R.56394	RCAF			†
	Sgt Melvin F. **Ramsey**	Can./ R.67828	(US)/RCAF			†
	Sgt Robert R. **Oliver**	Can./ R.75618	RCAF			†
24.09.42	Sgt Kenneth **Coates**	RAF No. 1006972	RAF	**AT233**	GX-B	†
	Sgt Dennis R. **Bird**	RAF No. 1382299	RAF			†
	Sgt Arthur H. **Gibbons**	RAF No. 1202136	RAF			†
	Sgt Arnold **Higson**	RAF No. 1122301	RAF			†
30.12.42	Sgt James C. **Donald**	Can./ R.105695	RCAF	**AE370**		-
	Alone on board					
26.02.43	*Caught fire and exploded while refuelling*	-	-	**P2065**		-
	Destroyed when P2065 exploded	-	-	**AE201**		-
23.03.43	W/C George H.D. **Evans**	RAF No. 33309	RAF	**AT232**	(GX)-A	-
	one another					**Inj.**
03.04.43	Sgt Donald **Montgomery**	Can./ R.101199	RCAF	**L4084**		†
	Sgt William J. **MacKay**	Can./ R.107062	RCAF			†
	Sgt John D. **Scott**	Can./ R.98256	RCAF			†
	Sgt John W. **Whipple**	Can./ R.105760	RCAF			†
24.04.43	F/Sgt James C. **Donald**	Can./ R.105695	RCAF	**AT244**	(GX)-M	†
	Sgt Cyril A. **Brown**	RAF No. 1098854	RAF			**Inj.**
	Sgt Allison **Glass**	Can./ R.86252	RCAF			**Inj.**
	Two cadet on boards, A. Birt and E. Gleaver were also injured.					
11.06.43	Sgt Frederick U. **Batchelor**	RAF No. 655429	RAF	**AT243**	(GX)-N	†
	Sgt Serge **Viatkin**	RAF No. 129409	RAF			†
	Sgt Eugene H. **Johnston**	Can./ R.105519	RCAF			†
	LAC Edgar J. **Dockendorff***	Can./ R.72726	RCAF			†
22.06.43	*Hit while parked by N9096. Destroyed*	-	-	**X3115**	(GX)-T	-
	See above. Damaged and SOC	-	-	**X3061**		-
06.09.43	P/O Robert E. **Ritscher**	Can./ J.14110	(US)/RCAF	**L4076**		†
	P/O Owen K. **Main**	Can./ J.20425	RCAF			†
	Sgt Howard J. **Hanson**	Can./ R.115118	RCAF			†
09.09.43	P/O Robert S. **Arnold**	Can./ J.13113	RCAF	**AD799**		†
	P/O Clyde E. **Coons**	Can./ J.14469	RCAF			†
	F/Sgt Donald K. **Stroud**	Can./ R.115118	RCAF			†

*Groundcrew

Total: 14

Ships claims - confirmed or probable: 1 *(ca. 4,000 tons)*
A/S patrols, hours flown: 380

First operational sortie:
01.05.42
Last operational sortie:
18.12.43

Number of sorties: 680

Total aircraft written-off: 28

Aircraft lost on operations: 14
Aircraft lost in accidents: 14

Squadron code letters:

UB *(up to end 1942)*

COMMANDING OFFICERS

W/C Grant M. LINDEMAN	RAF No. 37302	RAF	...	06.02.43
W/C Robert HOLMES	AUS. 406356	RAAF	06.02.43	05.12.43
W/C Jack N. DAVENPORT	AUS. 403403	RAAF	05.12.43	...

SQUADRON USAGE

Formed on 30 June 1941 as the first Australian bomber squadron, No. 455 Squadron began night operations on 29 August with its Hampdens. Night bombing operations continued until the squadron moved to Leuchars on 29 April 1942 and was placed under Coastal Command authority. The CO at the time was W/C G.M. Lindeman. At first it continued similar bombing and mining activities along the Norwegian coast on behalf of Coastal Command but, on 9 May, the first torpedo-bomber Hampdens arrived at the squadron: P2122, X3022, AE130, AE310, AE355 and AT109. All but AT109 were detached from No. 144 Squadron as a temporary measure. Other Hampdens were received, this time on a permanent basis: AE312 and AE442 on the 10th; L4038, AD736, AD836 on the 13th; and P2093, AD974, AE128, AE115 and AE296 the next day. By the end of the month, Hampdens L4118, P1150, P1153, P1245, P1287, P2100, P2126, P2145, P5304, P5323, P5315, P5327, X2904, AD799, AD865, AD908, AD976, AD977, AE156, AE194, AE201, AE307, AE435, AT114, AT131, AT150 and AT184 had been taken on charge, so 455 was now fully equipped with torpedo bombers (and a single remaining bomber). Training started at once; 16 operational bombing sorties were carried out in May. The training intensified during the summer with 550 hours flown in June and 500 in July. On 5 July, 12 Hampdens were dispatched for a first strike against an enemy naval vessel off Norway, the battleship *Tirpitz*, but the first box of six was intercepted by two Bf109s. Four of the Hampdens were hit by cannon and machine-gun fire, slightly injuring two airmen, but all aircraft returned to base safely without having found their target. This operation was repeated on the 9th but with no success. On 16 July, the squadron recorded its first major accident when X3150/U spun into the ground two-and-a-half miles from Leuchars during a training flight, killing the three crewmen on board. A single night strike was performed in August while the squadron began preparing to send a detachment to Vaenga in Russia. The detachment took off on 4 September but, as with No. 144 Squadron, things did not go well during the ferry flight: P5303/H crashed into Mount Arvestuottar, north of Arjeplog in Swedish Lappland (all five crew were killed); P5323/L crash landed due to fuel exhaustion at Kandalaksha, in the Kandalakshsky District of Murmansk, Russia, but the crew escaped major injury; AT109/C, flying in the dawn light, was damaged by flak from U-boat U-105 as it crossed the Arctic coast. It made a good forced landing on clear ground near the German fortress at Kiberg, on Malvik Beach near Vardø, Finnmark, Norway. The Germans took the Hampden by barge to Kirkennes; it was repaired and made at least one flight before being abandoned. In Russia, 455 flew its first torpedo sortie on the 14th but it was uneventful. On the 27th, the Australians lost a Hampden during an air raid; it was eventually reduced to spares. No further ops were carried out. The personnel embarked on HMS *Argonaut* on 23 October, leavings the Hampdens to the Soviets. In the meantime, the rest of the squadron at Leuchars continued to practice with the remaining aircraft but few hours were flown – less than 40 in September and more or less the same in October. However, at the end of October, ops resumed with two anti-submarine patrols flown on the 23rd. A few more were

Hampden AT137/UB-T during a training flight in May 1942. AT137 was issued to No. 455 Squadron at the end of 1941 and was coded 'C' (barred), until the original UB-T, P1203, was lost in action early in April 1942. AT137 was lost in a ground accident when it caught fire at Leuchars on 8 June 1942. Even though 455 was under Coastal Command authority at the time, it was still acting as a bomber squadron as it was still waiting for the assignment of aircraft converted to torpedo bombers. *(Andrew Thomas)*

achieved before the end of the month including using two Hampdens borrowed from 144 Squadron, 455 being short of aircraft. In November, the squadron tried to rebuild its Hampden fleet, only flying a single anti-submarine patrol for the month. It resumed its anti-shipping activities on 9 December when four Hampdens led by the CO were sent off against merchant shipping off the Norwegian coast; the op proved uneventful. Other night strikes followed and 455 recorded its first operational loss when P2078/P failed to return from such a flight on the 11th; the crew was posted missing. Two days later, the first torpedo drop was made by Sgt S.A. Vincent in AE314/L against a 2,000-ton ship off Norway. A hit was not observed. Another mishap was later recorded when, on the 22nd, AD836/B experienced a left engine failure shortly after take-off, forcing the pilot, W/O P.H. Baker, to make a forced landing in a wood near Leuchars. The crew was unhurt but the Hampden a total write-off. Then, on the 27th, AE378/G, flown by P/O MS Humphrey, managed to get in a good position to drop a torpedo against a 5,000-ton ship but, once more, no results could be observed. During the attack, an Ar196 engaged one of the Hampdens (AT249/C captained by P/O J.G.C. Oliver) but did not press home the advantage and the German pilot soon abandoned the chase after opening fire from 600 yards.

January 1943, apart from a change of CO, was a busy month with 12 ops performed, all but one being night-strike raids. The first raid was carried out on the 11th off the Norwegian coast. Hampden AN166/R could not participate as it experienced an engine failure after take-off obliging the pilot, Sgt S.A. Vincent, to put it down near Leuchars; Sgt D.T. Martin was killed and the three other crewmen injured to various degrees. This operation was one of misfortune as another Hampden had to return to base owing to engine trouble while P/O P.J. Hill's crew failed to return in AD792/P. A fourth Hampden was also obliged to land at Dyce, returning to Leuchars the next day. With regard to Hill's crew and AD792, it was discovered two days later they had crashed in remote country on the north side of the Hill of Warran, north of Edzell. Only Sgt R.K. Spohn, slightly injured, was able to extricate himself to seek assistance, walking about 40 hours before finding help. When the rescue team arrived at the crash site, however, they found two dead and Sgt R.A. Smithers seriously injured with a fractured leg. Sadly, it was too late to save the leg; it was amputated but Smithers succumbed to his wounds on the 19th. Losses continued to be recorded and, on the 25th, a full crew was posted missing in X3140/T after having ditched on the return leg from a day strike. On the credit side, one 2,000-ton vessel was hit by bombs on the 22nd (P/O Colin G Storry) but results were not observed. A U-boat was attacked with torpedoes and guns on the 27th. There was an exchange of fire with the Hampden (AE314/L, F/L A.H.G. Clarke), which fired 600 rounds, and the German gunners damaged the bomber in what was ultimately an inconclusive engagement. The squadron remained very active in February with more than 70 sorties carried out. While several attacks were made, no claims were forthcoming. On the other hand, no losses were recorded. March proved a busy month with over 80 sorties carried out, some being flown by attached No. 489 (NZ) Squadron crews. Ignoring several air-sea-rescue sorties, all the offensive sorties carried out with torpedoes produced no results. Anti-shipping strikes were performed with bombs, but no results were observed. Again, no operational losses were recorded during the month, but one Hampden crashed at Low Eldring while on a ferry flight from St. Athan to Leuchars. On 4 April, AT152/F was badly damaged by a BV138 while attacking a 6,000-ton ship off Norway. While the Hampden managed to drop its torpedo, no results were observed and it returned to base badly damaged where it crashed with two injured on board; it was duly written off. Otherwise, the rest of the month was uneventful even though various attacks were conducted, including on U-boats with depth charges, and a few torpedoes dropped. However, 455 came close to losing another Hampden when it was attacked by enemy fighters on the 12th. It escaped thanks to the violent evasive action taken by the pilot. While losses had been relatively light since the beginning of the year, May was a different story with the squadron seeing four of its Hampdens lost during practice flights or other non-operational activities. On 16 May, AN148/K was on a night training flight when it spun into sea off the Shetlands, killing the entire crew. Three days later, during another training flight, Sgt J.A. McDonald overshot his landing at Inverness in AD920, but fortunately no one was injured. Misfortune continued for 455 when it lost a third Hampden on the 24th when AT132/k collided with Beaufighter JL502 of No. 235 Squadron off Fraserburgh; all personnel were either killed or posted missing. May ended with the overshoot on take-off of AT150 at Leuchars, but this incident ended well for the crew. Also, on the 11th, AD979 had been wrecked when a No. 235 Sqn Beaufighter hit it while parked at Leuchars. On the operational side, 60 sorties were carried out but nothing was claimed for the effort. In June, operational activities were limited to 22 sorties across four uneventful operations. On 7 July, 455 carried out a major operation with a dozen Hampdens which headed to the Egers area. While two Hampdens returned home owing to engine trouble, with a third serving as escort, the remainder of the now-depleted formation continued to the target. The aircraft flown by S/L B.R.D. O'Connor was attacked by two Bf109s; one of them was probably hit by the rear gunner, but the other made five attacks before giving up, leaving the Hampden relatively unscathed thanks to O'Connor's skill in taking efficient evasive action. On 11 July, while on a practice flight, the right engine of AE228/P caught fire at 500 feet; the captain, F/O R.C. Barton, unable to return to base, made a crash landing a mile to the north, saving the crew from major injury. After a long time without any operational losses, Hampden AE146/N failed to return with its crew from a patrol off the Norwegian coast on 16 July. Generally speaking, though, July was a 'nothing' month; no ship was sighted. On 2 August, 455 claimed its first success when, off the Norwegian coast, a convoy consisting of a destroyer, two merchant ships and two flak ships was attacked by three Hampdens. While two of the torpedoes failed to drop (L4105/D and AE384/F), F/Sgt A.E Jones in P1346/T lined up on a 4,000-ton merchantman and successfully dropped his torpedo. The ship was hit and seen to be low in the stern; an explosion was also seen after the attack. It was later confirmed as having sunk. The flak, however, was far from inactive and Hampden L4105/D was badly damaged by one of the flak ships. While F/O I.H. Mason managed to get back to Leuchars, it was only to crash land the aircraft. Mason and his crew escaped injury, but the aircraft was eventually written off. Another Hampden was written off on the 11th while at Tain for a refresher torpedo course; L6090/J overshot a landing and was badly damaged. Three days later, AE378/G was posted missing from a shipping strike off Norway. The squadron remained active in the area until the end of the month. Various encounters occurred with German ships but no further claims were made. The Luftwaffe was also present and, on one occasion, a Ju88 attacked the Hampdens without success. Sadly, 455 would lose another Hampden in a training mishap on the 26th when AE195/M failed to return from a navigational exercise. It ditched after an engine failure and only one survivor was recovered. On 14 September, the squadron dispatched six Hampdens, in the usual two flights of three, for a day *Rover* off

Wing Commander Robert Holmes (left) commanded No. 455 Squadron for all of 1943 during the Hampden era. He was later repatriated to Australia and, from March 1945, commanded No. 13 Squadron RAAF flying Lockheed Venturas. On his left is Flight Lieutenant WA Branch, his adjutant.

Hampden P1164/UB-A during the summer of 1943. Note the undersurfaces are painted black instead of grey. *(AHM of WA)*

Norway. Only the second formation was fortunate to sight something. On making landfall near Lister, the Hampdens ran into extensive flak while inspecting a foundering ship. Continuing the patrol, they sighted four flak ships of about 800 tons each. The three Hampdens went in to attack and were immediately caught in the middle of heavy flak. Two of the bombers turned away to the right while AN157/N was seen commencing a turn away between a ship and the shore. Soon after, the crews of the other two Hampdens, which were now heading for base, observed a red/orange flash in the vicinity of the flak ships. The two crews presumed AN157/N had been shot down; indeed, it failed to return. The rest of the month proved uneventful with less than 30 sorties carried out. The squadron performed roughly the same number of sorties in October but suffered heavier losses: on the 7th, P1208/C went into a stabilised yaw soon after take-off and crashed, but the crew were unhurt; and P1207/P safely ditched out of fuel off Aberdeen during an air-sea-rescue sortie on the 27th. During the month, 455 had spent most of its time flying anti-submarine patrols. Despite the bad weather, it remained active in November; another Hampden, AN163/K, was lost on the 5th when it crashed on return from a Rover, fortunately without injuring the crew. This was the squadron's final operational Hampden loss. A few days later, on the 17th, P1246 crashed near Leuchars after an hydraulic failure during a training flight; no casualties were reported. Two days later, the long-awaited news finally arrived: 455 was soon to convert to the Beaufighter Mk.X. At the time, the last Hampdens in hands were L4075/D, P1166/M, P1236/G, P1246/V, P2080/J, P4312/Z, P5302/S, X2912/W, AD976/E, AE125/N, AE147/H, AE293/U, AE371/E, AE384/P, AE386/Y, AE387/B, AN149/X, AN157/N, AN161/Q, AN163/K. The final operational sorties on Hampdens occurred on 5 and 10 December with a new CO in command, W/C J.N. Davenport; all were uneventful. Training on Beaufighters commenced a few days later, but the Australians would use the Hampdens on an air-sea search for a missing BOAC Lodestar on the 18th.

Confiurmed claims against ships - 455 (RAAF) Squadron

Date	Captains	SN	Origin	tons	Serial	Code	Nb	Cat.
02.08.43	F/Sgt Arthur E. **Jones**	RAF No. 657461	RAF	4,000	**P1346**	T	1.0	C

Total: 1.0

Date	Crew	S/N	Origin	Serial	Code	Fate
27.09.42	*Damaged in air raid, not repaired*	-	-	**P2126**	UB-S	-
12.12.42	P/O Geoffrey I. **Gunton**	Aus. 403583	RAAF	**P2078**	UB-P	**PoW**
	P/O Thomas A. **Edgoose**	Aus. 404814	RAAF			†
	Sgt Douglas F. **Thomas**	Aus. 402779	RAAF			**PoW**
	Sgt Arnold E. **Crossley**	Aus. 404633	RAAF			†
22.12.42	W/O Philip H. **Baker**	RAF No. 1154323	RAF	**AD836**	UB-P	-
	F/Sgt Gordon S. **Dun**	Aus. 402568	RAAF			-
	Sgt Leslie A.H. **Jonas**	Aus. 400755	RAAF			-
	Sgt Noel **Bayliss**	Aus. 403583	(nz)/RAAF			-
11.01.43	Sgt Sydney A. **Vincent**	Aus. 403612	RAAF	**AD166**	(UB)-R	-
	F/Sgt Arthur L.W. **Watt**	Can./ R.86494	RCAF			-
	Sgt Kenneth C. **Applekamp**	Aus. 407634	RAAF			-
	Sgt Douglas T. **Martin**	Aus. 407681	RAAF			-
	P/O Philip J. **Hill**	RAF No. 122499	RAF	**AD792**	(UB)-P	†
	P/O William J. **Rees**	RAF No. 123457	RAF			†
	Sgt Reginald A. **Smithers**	Aus. 411656	RAAF			†
	Sgt Ronald K. **Spohn**	Aus. 412208	RAAF			†
25.01.43	P/O Eric J. **Gleeson**	Aus. 404707	RAAF	**X3140**	(UB-T	†
	P/O Kevin J. **Murphy**	Aus. 404766	RAAF			†
	Sgt Henry **Witte**	Aus. 404149	RAAF			†
	Sgt John R. **Booth**	Aus. 404395	RAAF			†
04.04.43	F/O Malcolm S. **Humphrey**	Aus. 400473	RAAF	**AT152**	(UB)-F	-
	F/O Dennis R. **Hawkes**	RAF No. 116451	RAF			-
	F/Sgt Thomas G. **Perry**	Aus. 407739	RAAF			-
	P/O Irving **Ackroyd**	Aus. 403548	RAAF			-
16.07.43	F/Sgt Sgt John A.R. **McDonald**	RAF No. 1388758	RAF	**AE146**	(UB)-N	**PoW**
	F/O John D. **Arthurell**	RAF No. 129410	RAF			**PoW**
	Sgt William E. **Ramsay**	Can./ R.121360	RCAF			**PoW**
	Sgt Lionel F.C. **Stewart**	Can./ R.109240	RCAF			**PoW**
02.08.43	F/O Ian H. **Masson**	RAF No. 127828	RAF	**L4105**	(UB)-D	-
	F/O Frederick J. **Skidmore**	RAF No. 129417	RAF			-
	F/O Jospeh B. **Mullan**	NZ416014	RNZAF			-
	F/O Garnett A. **Lennox**	Can./ J.13439	RCAF			-
14.08.43	P/O Vincent B.J. **Finn**	Aus. 411763	RAAF	**AE378**	(UB)-G	†
	F/O Richard T. **Latham**	RAF No. 124933	(aus)/RAF			†
	W/O Colin B. **Campbell**	Aus. 406431	RAAF			†
	F/Sgt Kenneth E. **Marriott**	RAF No. 551777	RAF			†
14.09.43	F/O William **Austin**	Aus. 402841	RAAF	**AN157**	(UB)-N	†
	F/Sgt John **Mellor**	RAF No. 655438	RAF			†
	F/Sgt Robert S.W. **Esmay**	Can./ R.114980	RCAF			†
	Sgt Eric W. **Smith**	RAF No. 1111788	RAF			†
07.10.43	F/Sgt Arthur E. **Jones**	RAF No. 657461	RAF	**P1208**	(UB)-C	-
	F/O Raymond R. **Lassiter**	RAF No. 129402	RAF			-
	F/Sgt James H. **Taylor**	Aus. 412753	RAAF			-
	F/Sgt Volney C. **Locker**	Aus. 412319	RAAF			-
27.10.43	F/O Thomas G. **Davis**	Aus. 420458	RAAF	**P1207**	(UB)-P	-
	F/O Albert O. **Peters**	Aus. 408874	RAAF			-
	F/Sgt Fred J.A. **Mechan**	Can./ R.135987	RCAF			-
	F/Sgt Donato A. **Vitarelli**	Can./ R.136141	RCAF			-

Date	Crew	S/N	Origin	Serial	Code	Fate
05.11.43	P/O Sydney J. **Cliff**	RAF No. 156701	RAF	**AN163**	(UB)-K	-
	F/O John C. **McGhee**	RAF No. 121251	RAF			-
	F/Sgt Douglas H. **McLean**	Can./ R.92022	RCAF			-
	Sgt James **MacFeeley**	RAF No. 982440	RAF			-

Total: 14

AT109/UB-C made a forced landing near Vardø en route to Vaenga. The crew was captured. (*Andrew Thomas Col.*)

Summary of the aircraft lost by accident - 455 (RAAF) Squadron

Date of TO	Crew	S/N	Origin	Serial	Code	Fate
08.06.42	*Caught fire on ground*	-	-	**AT137**	UB-T	-
04.09.42	Sgt Edward J. **Smart**	Aus. 404149	RAAF	**P5304**	UB-H	†
	Sgt Thomas G. **Nicholls**	Aus. 400331	RAAF			†
	Sgt Louis A. **Beggin**	RAF No. 1358006	RAF			†
	Sgt John M.O. **Harris**	Aus. 408129	RAAF			†
	Cpl Donald H. **Nelson***	Aus. 6707	RAAF			†

Date	Name	Number	Force	Aircraft	Code	Fate
	P/O Rupert B. **Patrick**	Aus. 403468	RAAF	**P5323**	UB-L	-
	Sgt Joseph C. **McIver**	Can./ R.72683	RCAF			-
	Sgt Reginald H. **Darnell**	Aus. 406520	RAAF			-
	Sgt Leo **Clohessy**	Aus. 406501	RAAF			-
	LAC Ronald R. **Bryans***	Aus. 11652	RAAF			-
	S/L James **Catanach**	Aus. 400364	RAAF	**AT109**	UB-C	**PoW**
	P/O George R. **Anderson**	Aus. 400316	RAAF			**PoW**
	F/Sgt Cecil W.F. **Cameron**	Aus. 404632	RAAF			**PoW**
	Sgt John R. **Hayes**	Aus. 404462	RAAF			**PoW**
	F/Sgt John D. **Davidson***	Aus. 5372	RAAF			**PoW**
27.03.43	Sgt John J. **O'Connor**	NZ415007	RNZAF	**AT184**	(UB-U	-
	Sgt Douglas G. **Simes**	NZ412751	RNZAF			-
	Sgt Richard E. **Wilson**	RAF No. 1206686	RAF			-
09.05.43	*Struck on ground by Beaufighter*	-	-	**AD979**	(UB)-M	-
16.05.43	F/Sgt Geoffrey V. **Courtney**	Aus. 411490	RAAF	**AN148**	(UB)-K	†
	F/O Alfred C. **Smith**	RAF No. 125634	RAF			†
	Sgt John A. **King**	RAF No. 1193308	RAF			†
	F/Sgt Charles H.A. **Smith**	Aus. 411627	RAAF			†
22.05.43	Sgt John A.R. **McDonald**	RAF No. 1388758	RAF	**AD920**	(UB)-H	-
	F/O John D. **Arthurell**	RAF No. 129410	RAF			-
	Sgt William E. **Ramsay**	Can./ R.121360	RCAF			-
	Sgt Lionel F.C. **Stewart**	Can./ R.109240	RCAF			-
24.05.43	F/Sgt John S. **Freeth**	Aus. 411768	RAAF	**AT132**	(UB)-K	†
	Sgt Albert J. **Wheatcroft**	RAF No. 13308014	RAF			†
	F/O Ian H. **Whitson**	Aus. 404593	RAAF			†
	F/Sgt Horace R.J. **Downing**	Can./ R.74871	RCAF			†
29.05.43	F/O Richard C. **Barton**	RAF No. 123155	RAF	**AT150**	(UB)-T	-
	Alone on board					
11.07.43	F/O Richard C. **Barton**	RAF No. 123155	RAF	**AE228**	(UB)-P	-
	Sgt Keir **McLaren**	RAF No. 1369722	RAF			-
	Sgt Elmer M. **Birkland**	Can./ R.121479	RCAF			-
16.07.43	Sgt Robert B.M. **Gemmel**	RAF No. 1343179	RAF	**X3150**	(UB)-U	†
	Sgt Arthur N. **Owen**	RAF No. 1334766	RAF			†
	F/O Winston F. **Bradshaw**	NZ412649	RNZAF			†
11.08.43	Sgt Geoffrey E. **Batchelor**	RAF No. 1338767	RAF	**L6090**	(UB)-J	-
	Sgt Kevin P. **Martin**	RAF No. 1389450	RAF			-
	Sgt Lorne S. **Guernsey**	Can./ R.123684	RCAF			-
	Sgt John R. **Anschetz**	Can./ R.131564	RCAF			-
26.08.43	Sgt Bertram C. **Woodroofe**	RAF No. 1558418	RAF	**AE195**	(UB)-M	†
	Sgt John P. **Taylor**	RAF No. 1317474	RAF			†
	Sgt Byron L. **Martin**	Can./ R.116081	RCAF			-
	Sgt Alexander G. **McKenzie**	Can./ R.130972	RCAF			†

*Groundcrew

Total: 14

AN148/K, returning from an early 1943 shipping strike, with its tail badly shot up by shipborne flak off Norway. Below, L4105/D was badly damaged by flak on 2 August 1943 and managed to return to Leuchars where it crash landed. All on board were unhurt.

Ships claims - confirmed or probable: 6 *(ca. 26,000 tons)*
A/S patrols, hours flown: 1,500

First operational sortie:
11.05.42
Last operational sortie:
26.10.43

Number of sorties: 780

Total aircraft written-off: 18

Aircraft lost on operations: 14
Aircraft lost in accidents: 4

Squadron code letters:

XA (up to end 1942)

COMMANDING OFFICERS

W/C James A.S. Brown	RAF No. 29060	RAF	...	19.10.42
W/C Victor C. Darling	RAF No. 33236	RAF	19.10.42	01.08.43
W/C John S. Dinsdale	RAF No. 40999	(NZ)/RAF	01.08.43	...

SQUADRON USAGE

On 12 August 1941, No. 489 (NZ) Squadron was formed under W/C J.A.S. Brown at Leuchars. It was intended to be equipped with Bristol Beauforts but by the end of the year only one was on charge due to supply issues. Therefore, early in January 1942, it was decided 489 would convert to Hampden torpedo bombers, which arrived in March 1942 at Thorney Island, the squadron's new home. In the meantime, while the Beaufort left, some intensive training was carried out with Blenheims. On 9 May, 489 sent a detachment to St. Eval and, two days later, the first anti-submarine patrols were carried out. Throughout the month, the squadron flew about 166 hours across about 30 patrols; all were uneventful if the short, inconclusive engagement with an He115 west of Brest on return from a patrol of the Spanish coast on the 22nd is ignored (AT233/P captained by F/O Willis). In June, while training continued at Thorney Island, other anti-submarine patrols were performed from St. Eval in the Bay of Biscay area up to the 24th. While no U-Boats were seen, 489 came close to losing a crew when P5335/R, captained by F/L R.G. Hartshorn, was intercepted by two Fw190s off Ushant on the 13th. The Hampden managed to get home with two wounded on board, Sgt J McGill-Brown and F/Sgt Dawnay (RAF), and the aircraft damaged by cannon and machine-gun fire. During the combat, one of the Fw190s was hit and broke off while the second continued to attack from different angles before finally disengaging. Shipping searches started on the 24th, and were repeated the next day, but nothing was sighted. In July, 489 sent various detachments to Abbotsinch and Wick while training continued at Thorney Island. During a flight on the 12th, the Hampden flown by F/O D.J. Nilsson hit the sea during a practice torpedo drop on the Firth of Clyde. The Hampden hit the water in a tail-down attitude and wings level, so the aircraft ditched relatively softly; the crew subsequently escaped with ease and were quickly picked up. Another Hampden was lost during a camera test flight ten days later; P1219/W crashed at sea but this time there were two casualties. On 14 July, off the Norwegian coast, the three Hampdens sent on a shipping recce sighted a convoy of merchant ships and one escort. They carried out an attack on the biggest merchant ship, but results were not observed. At the same time, they encountered a BV138 flying boat which engaged them in combat. The flying boat broke off and escaped in cloud after being hit in its right engine. This was the first shipping attack made by 489 Squadron Hampdens. No further operations were flown until 11 August due to preparations to move to, and the move itself, Skitten. That day, 11 August, twelve 489 Hampdens were directed to attack the cruiser *Lutzow*, believed to be heading south off the southern coast of Norway. No cruiser was found but S/L .C. Triptree and crew failed to return in P1337/M. In the first fortnight of September, 489 was mainly occupied with anti-submarine patrols from which AD795/K failed to return on the 14th. Three days later, during an anti-shipping strike, three Hampdens managed to find a convoy off the Norwegian coast, three miles west of Varhaug. The convoy consisted of one large merchant vessel of 6,000 tons, one of 2,000 tons and five escorts. Despite heavy flak, which hit one of the Hampdens, the three torpedoes were dropped and seen to hit the larger mer-

Above: Hampden AT259/XA-H in May 1942 during an anti-submarine patrol and, below, AT131/XA-V taken probably during a training flight as it didn't carry out any ops in May before the change of roundel style on the 27th. AT131 was lost soon after in a flying accident on 12 July but AT259 survived a few more months before it was shot by shipborne flak off Norway on 4 April 1943.

chant ship; all the ships were also strafed as much as possible to keep the flak gunners' heads down. The 6,000-tonner was claimed as sunk. October proved a month of less activity with only ten sorties flown for one loss and one claim. The claim was made off the Norwegian coast on the 21st against a convoy of one merchant ship of 3,000 tons escorted by a 600-tonner and a Ju88. The merchant ship was hit and probably sunk (the final results were not observed) and a brief skirmish with the Junkers took place before it entered cloud, probably to avoid being hit by its own flak. Then, one week later, P/O S.C. Carlson and crew failed to return from a shipping recce off Karmøy Island. Close to 60 sorties were carried out in November, 489 now operating with a new CO, W/C V.C. Darling, who had taken over on 19 October. Two convoy attacks were made on the 15th and the 25th and one merchant ship was claimed as probably sunk. Indeed, one of 4,000 tons was left listing to starboard (15th), while the attack on a 2,000-ton ship (25th) did not produce any observed results. On the debit side, a Hampden experienced engine trouble on the 25th and was obliged to return early to Skitten where it crashed. The crew escaped but the aircraft was destroyed by the subsequent fire. Despite unfavourable weather, 489 carried out about 40 sorties (anti-shipping strikes and anti-submarine patrols) in December. Another claim was made on the 9th with a merchant ship of 5,000 tons attacked and probably sunk. Other attacks on ships were achieved in December but no hits were noted.

January 1943's operations started on the 7th for 489 which carried out two patrols between Stornoway and the mainland while the first anti-shipping strike was flown four days later. No ships were seen. Other strikes followed and 489 sustained some losses: on the 18th, AT257/B failed to return when it was shot down by flak while attacking a convoy, the entire crew eventually becoming prisoners of war; On the 23rd, Hampden AN123/D was posted missing with its crew. The New Zealanders had their revenge on the 29th when they attacked a 3,000-ton merchant ship off Stavanger. The vessel was seen to sink by the stern. However, in February, despite close to 70 sorties being carried out, the usual mix of shipping strikes and anti-submarine patrols, no claim was made. At the same time, 489 sustained no loss. In March, the squadron was almost stood down, pending a move to Leuchars. Therefore, the first three weeks of March saw no flying. Then, as the squadron was not yet completely operational at Leuchars, several crews were attached to No. 455 Squadron for a couple of sorties from the 24th. The squadron resumed operations of its own on the 27th and, until the end of the month, a dozen sorties were carried out, including some convoy escorts during the last two days of March. On the 28th, four Hampdens were sent on a shipping recce in the Kristiansand area, but AT155/A had to return to base with engine trouble. The three remaining Hampdens continued their flight in formation when, suddenly, north of Rundo, AN156/K, captained by Sgt A Grant, which had fallen behind the formation, was seen to jettison its torpedo then try to climb before it spun into the sea and burst into flame. Despite appearances, only the pilot was killed; the other crew members survived as prisoners of war. In April, close to 70 sorties were performed and some successes recorded but they came at a high cost. On 4 April, AT259/W was hit by flak and dived into the sea while attacking a convoy off Trondheim; the squadron did not claim a hit. On 9 April, six Hampdens headed to the Norwegian coast on a shipping recce. Approaching the coast, a

AT255/XA-A, armed with a torpedo, on a Rover (anti-shipping patrol) during the summer of 1942. wearing the Coastal Command camouflage. Note the roundel under the wing, something unusual. AT255 was the last Hampden to return from an operation on 26 October 1943.

convoy of one 1,000-ton merchant vessel, another of 5,000 tons and a tanker of 5,000 tons was sighted. The convoy was escorted by two Arado 196 floatplane fighters. The Hampdens conducted their attack; AT253/P lining up on the tanker. It dropped its torpedo, which was seen to run true. The tanker exploded in vivid orange flames, followed by black smoke, and was claimed as sunk. AT258/T was seen to dive into the sea and blow up after attacking while P1189/K was seen with one engine smoking; nothing further was seen of this aircraft, but it was finished off by German fighters. No more enemy vessels were claimed during the month despite several attacks and two vessels, one of 2,000 tons and one of 3,000 tons, being hit on the 24th. The squadron sustained another loss on the 13th, however, when P1257/C failed to return from a shipping recce. The entire crew perished. With AT195/W falling victim to an accident during a training flight on the 3rd, April had been a bad month for the New Zealanders. May was another busy period. On the 4th, a 3–4,000 tonner was probably hit but its eventual fate was not observed. On the 13th, another convoy was attacked, Beaufighters from No. 404 Squadron RCAF serving as escort. This proved a good thing as German fighters, two Ju88s, were escorting the convoy. No claim was made, however. The next day, another convoy was attacked, still with no results, but P4304/X, probably hit by flak, was last seen with its left engine on fire. The crew was eventually captured. A few days later, P2084/O was posted missing from a shipping recce from Oberstadt to the Naze; this time, the crew perished. In all, about 80 sorties were carried out in May. In June, activity declined, with less than 60 sorties performed, but no loss was sustained. The fact that 489 carried out mainly anti-submarine patrols and air-sea-rescue flights during the month probably explained this as these duties, of course, usually did not expose the Hampdens to defensive fire from ships. The squadron returned to a more offensive role in July although some anti-submarine patrols were flown at the end of the month. Again, July was free of any major event if the wreck of X2905/T on the 28th from an engine failure on take-off from Tain for a training flight is ignored. The crew survived that incident. In August, Wing Commander Dinsdale, a New -Zealander serving in the RAF, took over 489. That month, the weather was mostly found to be unfavourable for anti-shipping operations; only four strikes were carried out off the Norwegian coast with one inconclusive attack made. The rest of the operations consisted of anti-submarine escorts, anti-submarine sweeps and air-sea-rescue work. On the first anti-shipping op, performed on 2 August, P1188/A was attacked by Fw190s and severely damaged soon after making landfall on the Norwegian coast. The pilot, W/O J Stain, managed to get back home to belly land his Hampden, still with the torpedo in the bomb bay as it could not be jettisoned for some reason; one of the crew, the rear gunner, was wounded during the fighter attack. The Hampden was not repaired, partly because of the severity of the damage sustained but also partly because of the pending withdrawal of the type. This was the squadron's last operational Hampden loss. The wea-

AN127/XA-Y, seen in July 1942, displays the new camouflage adopted at the time with Dark Sea Grey upper-surfaces and Sky undersurfaces. If the ORB is to be believed, the letter 'Y' was possibly painted as a hoax as it seems the aircraft never flew ops with this letter, instead wearing 'B' then 'C'. Also, the use of squadron codes was discontinued from Autumn 1942. Nevertheless, this new scheme was progressively introduced but, as far as the Hampden was concerned, the Sky was replaced by Night (black) to better hide the aircraft when the sun went down.

ther continued to hamper anti-shipping ops; half of the month saw no flying at all. Nevertheless, some anti-submarine patrols were carried out and there were two attacks on an enemy convoy on the 16th and the 19th but no results were forthcoming. At the beginning of October, 489 took part in an intensive anti-submarine effort in the area between the Faroes and Iceland and although no sightings were made, it was clear the U-boats were forced to remain submerged, and therefore slower, to avoid detection. In October, only two shipping strikes were carried out and one claim recorded. Early in the month, 489 was ordered to move back to Leuchars; this was completed on the 20th. It was from Leuchars that the last operational Hampden sorties were carried out on the 26th when a shipping strike produced an inconclusive attack on a 6,000-ton vessel. Soon after, conversion to the Beaufighter TF.X commenced.

Confiurmed claims against ships - 489 (NZ) Squadron

Date	Captains	SN	Origin	tons	Serial	Code	Nb	Cat.
17.08.42	F/Sgt Arthur E. **Jones**	RAF No. 657461	RAF	6,000	**P1346**	T	1.0	C
21.10.42	F/O James J. **Richardson**	NZ404947	RNZAF	3,000	**AT257**	B	1.0	P
15.11.42	W/O Ralph C. **Dunn**	NZ404997	RNZAF	4,000	**AD855**	Y	1.0	C
09.12.42	F/Sgt John **Strain**	RAF No. 740003	RAF	5,000	**AT256**	G	1.0	P
29.01.43	S/L George H.D. **Evans**	RAF No. 33309	RAF	3,000	**AT252**	S	0.33	C
	F/O Denis W. **Wheeler**	RAF No. 121416	RAF		**AT258**	T	0.33	C
	F/O Charles J. **Freshney**	NZ405250	RNZAF		**AT259**	W	0.33	C
04.04.43	F/O Selwyn **Latta**	NZ41339	RNZAF	5,000	**AT253**	P	1.0	C

Total: 6.0

Armed with torpedoes, two of No. 489 Squadron's Hampdens head to the Norwegian coast at sea level. Hampden 'L' is probably AD979 as this aircraft was allocated this letter for most of 1943. Previously, it had been used by L4145.

Date (TO)	Crew	S/N	Origin	Serial	Code	Fate
11.08.42	S/L Alan C. **Triptree**	RAF No. 33349	RAF	P1337	XA-M	†
	F/L John J. **Hurley**	RAF No. 66003	RAF			†
	Sgt Jeffrey O. **Wellard**	RAF No. 934712	RAF			†
	Sgt George H. **Jones**	NZ405490	RNZAF			†
14.09.42	F/O Thomas D.G. **Murray**	NZ404925	RNZAF	AD795	XA-K	†
	Sgt Charles C. **Brandon**	NZ404958	RNZAF			†
	Sgt Douglas **Newman**	NZ41602	RNZAF			†
	Sgt Alexander G. **Brown**	NZ41568	RNZAF			†
28.10.42	P/O Stanley C.W. **Carlson**	RAF No. 117445	RAF	AT251	XA-O	†
	Sgt Stuart J. **Vincent**	RAF No. 1316950	RAF			†
	P/O Jack B. **Lawrence**	RAF No. 122558	RAF			†
	Sgt Henry G.N. **Fisher**	Can./ R.92204	RCAF			†
25.11.42	F/Sgt John **Dubbury**	RAF No. 917578	RAF	AT238	XA-O	-
	F/Sgt James F. **Lavin**	NZ405547	RNZAF			-
	P/O Dennis K. **Simmans**	Can./ J.15404	RCAF			-
	F/Sgt Glen R. **Burt**	NZ404630	RNZAF			-
18.01.43	F/O James J. **Richardson**	NZ404947	RNZAF	AT257	(XA)-B	PoW
	F/Sgt Colin B. **McKenzie**	NZ402920	RNZAF			PoW
	F/Sgt Albert A. **Hyde**	NZ404639	RNZAF			PoW
	Sgt Guy A. **Gaskill**	NZ404600	RNZAF			PoW
23.01.43	P/O William C. **Salmond**	Aus. 411668	RAAF	AN123	(XA)-D	†
	Sgt John H. **Sheppard**	RAF No. 1286391	RAF			†
	F/Sgt James **Maguire**	Can./ R.106115	RCAF			†
	F/Sgt Alfred G.G. **Brown**	Can./ R.92108	RCAF			†
28.03.43	F/Sgt Allen **Grant**	RAF No. 655391	RAF	AN156	(XA)-K	†
	Sgt Walter C. **Nicholson**	RAF No. 1391371	RAF			PoW
	Sgt Frederick J. **Brotherton**	RAF No. 1376315	RAF			PoW
	Sgt Robert **Holloway**	RAF No. 1286134	RNZAF			PoW
04.04.43	F/O Charles J. **Freshney**	NZ405250	RNZAF	AT259	(XA)-W	†
	F/Sgt William P. **Lanigan**	NZ405246	RNZAF			†
	Sgt Ronald L. **Ward**	RAF No. 1250955	RAF			†
	F/Sgt Frederick W. **Bacon**	NZ403752	RNZAF			†
09.04.43	F/O Denis W. **Wheeler**	RAF No. 121416	RAF	P1189	(XA)-K	†
	Sgt Geoffrey H. **Smith**	RAF No. 1575324	RAF			†
	F/O Leo N. **Selthun**	Can./ J.11122	RCAF			†
	F/Sgt Andrew B. **McDonald**	Can./ R.11934	RCAF			†
	F/O Selwyn **Latta**	NZ41339	RNZAF	AT258	(XA)-T	†
	F/O Sydney H. **Wolpole**	RAF No. 120137	RAF			†
	Sgt John **McAllister**	RAF No. 1052442	RAF			†
	F/Sgt Wallace J. **Douglas**	NZ403618	RNZAF			†
13.04.43	F/O Anthony E.B. **Barnard**	RAF No. 102065	RAF	P1257	(XA)-C	†
	W/OI Frederick M. **Holobow**	Can./ R.77570	RCAF			†
	F/Sgt William J. **McElrich**	NZ405500	RNZAF			†
	Sgt Ivan **Griffiths**	NZ405486	RNZAF			†
14.05.43	P/O John **Dubbery**	RAF No. 142851	RAF	P4304	(XA)-X	PoW
	F/Sgt Arthur H. **Jones**	NZ404374	RNZAF			PoW
	F/Sgt Douglas A. **Brier**	NZ403755	RNZAF			PoW
	F/Sgt Glen R. **Burt**	NZ404630	RNZAF			PoW
19.05.43	F/Sgt Reginald W. **Easton**	RAF No. 1214326	RAF	P2084	(XA)-O	†

	Sgt Edward M. **Whitsed**	RAF No. 655609	RAF			†
	F/Sgt Gerald J. **McEachern**	Can./ R.61464	RCAF			†
	Sgt John R. **Keeping**	Can./ R.98537	RCAF			†
02.08.43	W/O John **Strain**	RAF No. 740003	RAF	**P1188**	(XA)-A	-
	F/O Edmund F.J. **Fordham**	RAF No. 135445	RAF			-
	W/O Hugo R.F. **Smith**	NZ403759	RNZAF			-
	F/Sgt James F. **Marks**	NZ415546	RNZAF			-

Total: 14

Three of No. 489 Squadron's Hampdens in formation in late 1942. AT252/S is leading while AT147/X and P5335/R are close behind. The squadron had recently dropped the squadron codes; the overpainted 'XA' can be seen on AT252.

Date (TO)	Crew	S/N	Origin	Serial	Code	Fate
12.07.42	F/O Douglas J. **NILSSON**	NZ404929	RNZAF	**AT131**	XA-V	-
	P/O Hugh W. **COWAN**	RAF No. 67107	RAF			-
	Sgt JP **SCOTT**	?	?			-
	Sgt Leslie R. **LANDER**	NZ405495	RNZAF			-
22.07.42	F/O Peter E. **DANIELS**	RAF No. 66537	RAF	**P1219**	XA-W	-
	P/O Jack B. **LAWRENCE**	RAF No. 122558	RAF			-
	F/Sgt Brian J.D. **WARDE**	RAF No. 754755	RAF			†
	LAC Leslie **RICHES**	RAF No. 1280938	RAF			†
	LAC James J. **GAITENS**	RAF No. 646644	RAF			†
03.04.43	F/Sgt Stanley C. **PRICE**	RAF No. 1262749	RAF	**AT195**	(XA)-W	-
	Rest of the crew unrecorded					
28.07.43	F/O Brinley E. **STOURTON**	RAF No. 123025	RAF	**X2905**	(XA)-T	-
	Alone on board					

*Groundcrew

Total: 4

Worth noting, the presence of a Dane with 489 Sqn, Flying Officer Henning Pedersen. Working fro Danish Air Lines in London when war broke out, he enlisted in the RAF November 1940, he joined 489 in August 1942 and served with 489 until February 1943 when he was posted to No 144 Squadron. He is here on front of his regular mount, AN154/K. He survived the war

October 1942, AE261/C leads AT225/A (now with squadron codes removed) and another Hampden during a training flight. No torpedoes are carried. Note the paint square behind the fuselage roundel showing the location of the overpainted squadron codes.

AD852/N wearing the new camouflage scheme in early 1943. The undersurfaces are black.

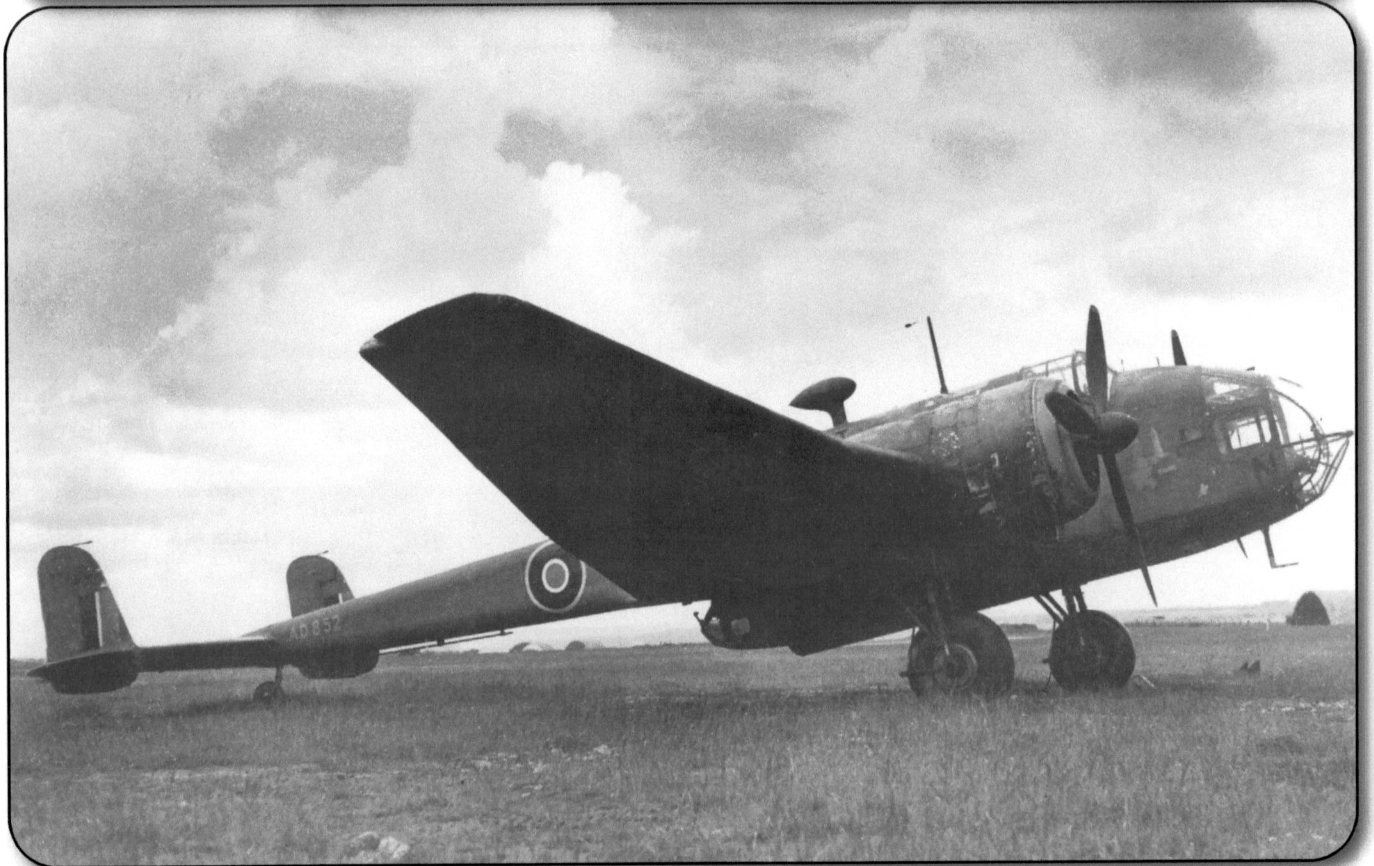

Ignoring trial units, the Hampden torpedo bomber was used by several main non-combat units:
-       No. 5 (C) OTU was initially formed to train Beaufort crews in August 1941. When the Hampden was introduced to Coastal Command, the size of the unit was increased by 36 aircraft plus 11 in reserve in May 1942. However, most of these Hampdens were conventional bombers and provided only basic training on the type. In November 1942, to increase torpedo training, a section equipped with Hampden torpedo bombers was detached to the Torpedo Training Unit (TTU), also located at Turnberry, where it eventually merged into No. 1 TTU on 1 January 1943. The 5 OTU establishment was subsequently reduced to nine Hampdens, plus one in reserve, which were stricken during the autumn pending the withdrawal of the type. Even though a handful of Hampden torpedo bombers continued to be used, it was only for basic training on the type, the capacity for torpedo training being irrelevant.
-       No. 1 Torpedo Training Unit used the type for a year between January 1943 and January 1944. It was formed on 1 January 1943 by absorbing torpedo elements of No. 5 (C) OTU at Turnberry. Various types were used but, in April, 1 TTU had an official establishment of eight Hampden torpedo bombers plus two in reserve. By November, while the type was being withdrawn, this establishment was cut by half before totally disappearing during January 1944. During the year, five major accidents on Hampdens were recorded.
-       No. 32 (C) OTU, which was formed in the UK in July 1941, embarked for Canada the same month. In August, it arrived on the west coast at Patricia Bay in British Columbia and began to reform. Its task was at first to train general-reconnaissance crews; this later changed to anti-shipping crews. In October, Beauforts were taken on charge. The first Hampdens were received on 16 May 1942 with the arrival of the first three (AN141, AN143 and AN147). At first, regarding the Hampdens, the official establishment was given as 28 airframes but, at the end of August, only 25 were on hand. Strength on paper was raised to 50 in September but it was not until Autumn 1943, with the arrival of 22 Hampdens from the UK taken on charge in the September–November period, that numbers on hand approached this figure. Indeed, the unit experienced a high accident rate and, coupled with a poor rate of serviceability, could only count an average of 50% daily availability, sometimes less (a third). From the start, the Hampdens should have been equipped with the torpedo kit, but these were slow to arrive and it was not until the autumn of 1942 that all the aircraft had the correct slings. The Hampdens were used until 21 February 1944 when the last of the 46 still on hand at the end of January left; the unit flew more than 32,600 hours on the type.

Summary of the aircraft lost by accident - TTU/1 TTU

Date	Crew	S/N	Origin	Serial	Code	Fate
12.10.42	Sgt Gareth **HOWELL**	RAF No. 1282866	RAF	**AN151**		†
	P/O William T. **WALTON**	RAF No. 125309	RAF			†
	Sgt Stanley W. **SHADRACK**	RAF No. 1385558	RAF			†
	Sgt Ernest W. **EVANS**	NZ411751	RNZAF			†
18.04.43	Sgt Ronald S. **CORDINGLEY**	RAF No. 1147967	RAF	**AT125**		†
	Sgt Eric **VEVERS**	RAF No.1149744	RAF			†
	Sgt John B. **REID**	CAN./ R.114641	RCAF			†
03.05.43	Sgt Leslie F. **PARRATT**	RAF No. 1289414	RAF	**AT117**		†
	F/O John H.B. **EYLES**	RAF No. 129407	RAF			†
07.08.43	F/O John H.W. **JOHNSTONE**	AUS. 414043	RAAF	**X3026**		†
	Sgt Eric D. **LEE**	AUS. 414413	RAAF			†
	Sgt Sidney R. **GREER**	NZ417208	RNZAF			†
	Sgt Leslie N. **BUTTIMORE**	NZ417194	RNZAF			†
16.08.43	Sgt John R. **MAXWELL**	AUS. 420624	RAAF	**P5341**		-
	Sgt Ronald G. **WARFIELD**	AUS. 414111	RAAF			-
	Sgt Leslie E. **STENCIL**	AUS. 414965	RAAF			-
	Sgt Alan D. **RIORDAN**	AUS. 420489	RAAF			†

Total: 5

No. 1 TTU used numerals to identify its aircraft. Here '118' is seen during a training flight.

Summary of the aircraft lost by accident - 32 OTU

Date	Crew	S/N	Origin	Serial	Code	Fate
10.06.42	P/O John M. **IRELAND**	RAF No. 122500	RAF	**AN143**		-
	Solo flight					
03.07.42	P/O George R. **DAVIES**	RAF No. 122463	RAF	**AN109**		-
	P/O Arthur F. **BOYD**	RAF No. 123097	RAF			-
	P/O Leo N. **SELTHUN**	CAN./ J.11122	RCAF			-
	Sgt Harold E. **BOWMAN**	CAN./ R.102132	RCAF			-
10.07.42	Sgt Edward **WILLIAMSON**	RAF No. 1080657	RAF	**AJ989**		-
	Sgt Alan F. **VAUGHAN**	RAF No. 1387341	RAF			-
	Sgt Archibald P. **McKINNON**	NZ412246	RNZAF			-
	Sgt Cyril F. **JOHNSON**	NZ413759	RNZAF			-
05.08.42	Sgt Jeffrey M. **McCARRISON**	NZ414646	RNZAF	**P5400**		-
	Solo flight					
04.10.42	P/O Norris **THOMAS**	RAF No. 49136	RAF	**AN105**		†
	Solo flight					
25.10.42	Sgt John **ORRELL**	RAF No. 1232301	RAF	**AJ988**		†
	Sgt Henry J. **THORN**	RAF No. 1315905	RAF			†
26.10.42	Sgt Thomas **JONES**	RAF No. 1088816	RAF	**AN128**		-
	Sgt Ronald S. **DARTNELL**	RAF No. 1292999	RAF			-
	Sgt Edward T.A. **HARRINGTON**	CAN./ R.114387	RCAF			-
	Sgt Bert J. **TUCKER**	CAN./ R.106659	RCAF			-

Date	Name	Service No	Air Force	Aircraft	
15.11.42	Sgt Leonard H. **Robinson**	RAF No. 1314375	RAF	**P5436**	-
	Sgt Derick W. **Smith**	RAF No. 1270519	RAF		-
	Sgt Kennth E. **Blood**	Aus. 412370	RAAF		-
	Sgt Jean O.F. **Fink**	Can./ R.90519	RCAF		
25.11.42	Sgt Frank **Cuss**	RAF No. 656246	RAF	**AN144**	-
	Solo flight				
30.11.42	Sgt Harry R. **Clasper**	RAF No. 909307	RAF	**AN140**	-
	Sgt Douglas J. **Cartridge**	RAF No. 1334770	RAF		-
	Sgt Alexander D.McB. **Donald**	Can./ R.83657	RCAF		
	Sgt Maurice L. **Parker**	Can./ R.121841	RCAF		
02.12.42	Sgt Bertram C. **Woodroofe**	RAF No. 1558418	RAF		-
	Solo flight				
24.01.43	Sgt John H. **Thomas**	RAF No. 1435349	RAF	**AN110**	-
	Sgt James E. **Ankerson**	RAF No. 1318208	RAF		-
	Sgt Alexander **Kasakewigh**	Can./ R.86752	RCAF		-
24.02.43	Sgt Philip O.H. **Herbert**	RAF No. 1315297	RAF	**P5431**	-
	Solo flight				
14.03.43	P/O Allan W.J. **Hunt**	Aus. 420343	RAAF	**P5433**	†
	P/O Reginald K. **Manttan**	Aus. 414416	RAAF		†
	P/O Grant L. **Hall**	Can./ J.22085	RCAF		†
	Sgt Howard S. **Piercy**	Can./ R.129632	RCAF		†
16.03.43	P/O Santiago S. **Lindsey**	Can./ J.13636	RCAF	**AN145**	-
	Sgt Walter N. **Stephens**	RAF No. 122289	RAF		-
	Sgt John J. **Hayes**	Can./ R122018	RCAF		-
	Sgt Lorne A. **Kennedy**	Can./ R95605	RCAF		-
13.04.43	P/O James S. **Peterkin**	RAF No. 135517	RAF	**AN121**	†
	Sgt Richard T. **Barrow**	Aus. 421149	RAAF		†
	Sgt Donald D. **MacGallivray**	Can./ R.139766	RCAF		†
	Sgt Keith E. **Thompson**	Can./ R.166015	RCAF		-
15.04.43	Sgt Donald **Nixon**	RAF No. 1438315	RAF	**AN133**	-
	Sgt Allan J. **Sargent**	Aus. 410098	RAAF		-
	Sgt Robert **Meyer**	Can./ R.141616	RCAF		-
	Sgt Russell **Urban**	Can./ R. 125893	RCAF		-
26.04.43	Sgt John T. **Hynes**	Aus. 414690	RAAF	**P5434**	-
	Solo flight				
06.05.43	P/O William **Marsden**	RAF No. 151059	RAF	**AN114**	-
	Solo flight				
18.05.43	Sgt Peter M. **Griffiths**	RAF No. 1339361	RAF	**AN113**	-
	Solo flight				
	Sgt John **Birch**	RAF No. 1323617	RAF	**AN135**	-
	Solo flight				
23.05.43	P/O Charles J. **Davis**	Aus. 420684	RAAF	**AN142**	†
	Sgt Alan R. **Marlow**	RAF No. 1577871	RAF		†
	Sgt Reginald J. **Hugues**	Aus. 422565	RAAF		†
	Sgt Colin L. **Bishop**	Aus. 418499	RAAF		†
	(Sgt Bishop actually died of wounds four days later)				
27.05.43	Sgt Geoffrey A. **Webster**	RAF No. 1438569	RAF	**AJ991**	-
	Sgt Kenneth **Rowling**	RAF No. 1239550	RAF		-
	Sgt Herbert E. **Hollitt**	Aus. 417465	RAAF		-
	Sgt Leslie R. **Coghlan**	Aus. 410872	RAAF		-
04.06.43	Sgt William F. **Barker**	RAF No. 961519	RAF	**AN100**	†
	Sgt Jack **Ralph**	RAF No. 1395495	RAF		†
	Sgt George W. **Maddrell**	Aus. 422214	RAAF		†
	Sgt Grant C. **Senger**	Aus. 418185	RAAF		†
14.06.43	F/O George C. **Douglas-Home**	RAF No. 126996	RAF	**AJ992**	†
	P/O Charles **Sudgen**	RAF No. 151391	RAF		†
	Sgt Alan S. **Lynch**	Aus. 420751	RAAF		†
	Sgt Elton R. **Ritchie**	Aus. 421626	RAAF		†

Date	Name	Service No.	Air Force	Aircraft	
23.07.43	P/O James B.A. **Thompson**	Aus. 425391	RAAF	**AJ996**	-
	P/O Arthur W. **Lockwell**	RAF No. 151681	RAF		-
	Sgt Kenneth R. **Bruce**	Aus. 422400	RAAF		
	Sgt Noel R. **Chaffrey**	Aus. 421711	RAAF		
	P/O Cecil A. **McPherson**	Aus. 413321	RAAF	**AN102**	
	P/O Edwin J. **Lipscombe**	RAF No. 151683	RAF		
	Sgt David J. **Davies**	Aus. 422539	RAAF		
	Sgt William M. **Christie**	Aus. 421246	RAAF		
27.07.43	P/O John R.M. **Ramshaw**	RAF No. 151137	RAF	**P5421**	-
	Solo flight				
31.07.43	F/O Paul A. **Hartman**	Can./ J.8419	RCAF	**P5427**	-
	Solo flight				
10.08.43	Sgt Glyn **Williams**	RAF No. 1488695	RAF	**AJ990**	-
	Solo flight				
12.08.43	P/O Albert **Shippin**	RAF No. 151548	RAF	**AJ995**	-
	Sgt James H. **Oblein**	RAF No. 1602241	RAF		-
	Sgt William A. **Park**	Aus. 422679	RAAF		-
	Sgt David J. **Oliver**	Aus. 422671	RAAF		-
18.08.43	P/O Ronald K. **Westhorp**	RAF No. 151647	RAF	**AN141**	-
	P/O Kenneth H. **Webster**	RAF No. 151838	RAF		-
	F/Sgt James M. **Booth**	Can./ R.93200	RCAF		-
	F/Sgt John A. **Buckhan**	Can./ R.121780	RCAF		-
04.09.43	Sgt John R. **Baillie**	RAF No. 1561964	RAF	**AJ998**	-
	Solo flight				
05.09.43	*Ground accident*	-	-	**P5429**	-
16.09.43	P/O Edward J. **Stainer**	RAF No. 152330	RAF	**P5399**	-
	Solo flight				
17.09.43	Sgt Alec W.V. **Fear**	RAF No. 1268737	RAF	**AN146**	†
	Solo flight				
19.09.43	P/O Harry H. **Frost**	Can./ J.24373	RCAF	**AJ993**	†
	Sgt Albert S. **Dobie**	RAF No. 1324459	RAF		†
	F/Sgt Albert **France**	Can./ R.113346	RCAF		†
	F/Sgt John R. **Bateman**	Can./ R.103889	RCAF		†
28.09.43	Sgt Herbert D. **McLeod**	NZ405556	RNZAF	**AJ994**	†
	Solo flight				
09.10.43	P/O Allen L. **Warner**	RAF No. 151706	RAF	**AN101**	†
	P/O Kenneth **Shaw**	RAF No. 152316	RAF		†
	Sgt Francis K. **Maiden**	Aus. 423799	RAAF		†
	Sgt Neville O. **Weekes**	Aus. 413700	RAAF		†
15.10.43	P/O Lionel J. **Thrift**	Aus. 422758	RAAF	**L4145**	-
	Solo flight				
16.10.43	Sgt Ronald F. **Allcorn**	RAF No. 1318169	RAF	**AN132**	†
	Sgt Peter F. **Hornbrook**	RAF No. 1586882	RAF		†
	Sgt Raymond R.G. **Porter**	Aus. 21526	RAAF		†
	Sgt Mervyn C.B. **Smith**	Aus. 423098	RAAF		†
10.11.43	P/O James E.L. **Gilmore**	Aus. 426085	RAAF	**P5424**	-
	Sgt John F. **Bishop**	RAF No. 1396510	RAF		-
	Sgt Walter T. **Elliot**	Aus. 426340	RAAF		-
	Sgt Roger J. **Chartrand**	Can./ R.106424	RCAF		-
30.11.43	Sgt James F. **Fearnley**	RAF No. 999804	RAF	**AN131**	†
	Sgt Leslie **Pettit**	RAF No. 1600923	RAF		†
13.01.44	Sgt Roland **Hayes**	RAF No. 1604260	RAF	**AD767**	†
	Solo flight				
14.01.44	Sgt Harold C. **Birch**	RAF No. 1582821	RAF	**AN136**	†
	Solo flight				
21.01.44	Sgt John S.T.J. **Budgen**	RAF No. 1525492	RAF	**AN122**	†
	Solo flight				

28.01.44	Sgt Ronald F.I. **Watson**	RAF No. 1604441	RAF	**P1200**	†
	P/O William R. **Dishman**	RAF No. 154274	RAF		†
	Sgt Edward G. **Quigley**	Can./ R.191291	RCAF		†

Total: 46

Above, P5428/HK during a solo training flight. This was another Hampden which was victim of an accident. It stalled on landing on 24.10.42, but the pilot escaped injury and the aircraft was eventually repaired.

Below, AN118/HAM survived its long career at No. 32 OTU. As with most of the surviving Hampdens in Canada, it was eventually struck off charge on 2 August 1944.

Above, AJ993/HAP in the mud after an incident on 2 February 1943. It was later lost with its crew when it dived into the sea in poor visibility on 19 September. Below, AJ991/HAN of No. 32 OTU dropping a practice torpedo. It was wrecked in May 1943 during an overshoot on landing. The crew escaped unhurt.

Handley Page Hampden Mk. I AE201
No. 415 (RCAF) Squadron
Wick (UK), summer 1942

Handley Page Hampden Mk. I P1164
No. 455 (RAAF) Squadron
Leuchars (UK), autumn 1942

Handley Page Hampden Mk. I AD852
No. 489 (NZ) Squadron
Wick (UK), summer 1943

SQUADRONS! - The series

SQUADRONS!
No.54
Phil H. LISTEMANN
The Hawker
Biplane Fighters
AT WAR:
STUDY, HISTORY AND STATISTICS
No.137 Squadron
1941 - 1945
COMPILED BY
H. LISTEMANN
WITH
CHRIS THOMAS
USN AIRCRAFT
1922-1962
Vol.7:
signation Letter
F' (Pt-4)
NN
James Edgar JOHNSON DSO** DFC
Supermarine Spitfire Mk.XIV MV257
No. 125 Wing
Group Captain J. E. Johnson
RAF No. 83267
B.160/Kastrup (Denmark), June 1945
WWW.RAF-IN-COMBAT.com
- USN Aircraft 1922-1962 -
- Squadrons! -
- RAF, Dominion and Allied squadrons at War -
- Allied Wings -
- Fighter Leaders -
- Prints (Aces and Leaders) -
Fighter Leaders
Volume VII
Phil H. Listemann
ALLIED WINGS
No.19
Electric CANBERRA
SQUADRON
No.17
Phil H. LIST
The Curtiss
Mohawk

9 782494 471160